Small Business Veteran

MY JOURNEY FROM LAMBEAU FIELD
TO THE WHITE HOUSE

Mr. Kbs,
Thnk yu fo speaking t my
Crp AGAIN! Sorg chat u AC!

Advantage™
BOOKS

[signature]

SHAUN G. BRADLEY

CO-FOUNDER OF BRADLEY-MORRIS, INC.

ISBN: 978-1-59755-388-9

Published by: ADVANTAGE BOOKS™
Longwood, Florida, USA
www.advbookstore.com

Library of Congress Catalog Number: 2016932035

First Printing: February 2016
16 17 18 19 20 21 22   10 9 8 7 6 5 4 3 2 1
Printed in the United States of America

To Libby,

For believing in me.

Shaun G. Bradley

Table of Contents

PROLOGUE

On November 17, 2007, I sold my interest in Bradley-Morris, Inc (BMI), the company I cofounded with Sandy Morris in 1991. That night, consumed with memories, and after the laughter and fun of my retirement party had died down, I wrote down some things I learned along the way and thought were important, while they were still fresh in my mind.

While many of them formed the basis for this book, I never really had any intention of writing one. I just didn't want to forget what I had learned and seen work. Now, as time has passed, it seems right. I have been encouraged by many of my former people in letters, as well as in conversations over the years, telling me how BMI impacted their lives. So many suggested I should write a book, that I feel some responsibility to them to do this. The term Shangri-La was used more than a few times to describe our time together at BMI. Many of their stories centered on the fun we had or how much they felt I cared about them. The stories about me caring are true, because I did.

In the spring of 2014, I experienced a life-changing event when my wife, Libby, nearly died three separate times from surgery-caused septic shock. She spent 35 days in an Intensive Care Unit (ICU) in a medically induced coma, followed by months of recovery. She is in the five-percent club that recovers fully, but it was a very close call. The BMI story was hers, too, and I wanted to tell it.

No doubt, BMI was very special. There was great camaraderie, and we were very successful. People grew and accomplished things beyond their wildest dreams. Not all stayed, but even those who left, viewed their time at BMI as setting a standard that helped them be successful wherever they went. Most missed BMI. As legendary University of Michigan Football Coach Bo Schembechler said, "The Team, The Team, The Team." We did it together. However, this book includes more about me than I am really comfortable sharing, but I knew I needed to get past that to tell this story.

A lot of what I've written about will probably seem like second nature to people in well-established companies, but somewhere and at some point, the processes, methods and culture in those companies were created. This book provides a window into how this was accomplished at BMI from creation to success, through expansion and setbacks, and then to success once again.

CHAPTER 1

Introduction

While I had personal conversations with most of my people telling them of my retirement plans, just before leaving my office for the final time, I sent the following note to all of the great people at BMI. What a ride it was!

All,

I began my career in military recruiting just over 20 years ago. I showed up in Atlanta driving a Ryder truck, which towed a Pontiac Grand Prix. I didn't know a soul, and had never met my new boss, save for a telephone conversation. I met my wife, Libby, the first day, and then met Sandy on the first day of training. (Yes, Sandy trained me.) Sometimes you just get lucky.

Since that time, I've had two stints in our world, Lucas[1] and BMI, and have built a wonderful life here. As the original military hire for Lucas Atlanta, in some respects you might say I was one of the originals who were on the lead wave that changed our industry from small shops of four to five people to what it has now become. Although the former Career Development guys (Terry, Tom, Ben and Mike)[2] are the real originals and, in many ways, set the mark

---

[1] The Lucas Group. National staffing firm headquartered in Atlanta.

[2] Career Development Corporation. Military recruiting firm located outside of Washington, DC. BMI would eventually acquire them. Terry Jemison, Tom Wolfe, Ben Labalbo and Mike McGovern were the owners.

for what I hoped to become. The time has now come to close the BMI Chapter of my life.

Make no mistake. This is not easy for me, as I've become very close to many of you over the years. Many of you know of my relationship with Rear Admiral "Mitch" Mitchell, who along with my high school basketball coach, is the biggest non-family influence of my life. We were together almost every day for two years, and when he rotated off of our aircraft carrier, he said he hoped he had communicated to us on a daily basis how much we meant to him. I now understand what he meant.

My work here is done. I am of a generation, which earned its spurs before answering machines were even in existence. Sandy and I started BMI 16 years ago with dreams that have been realized. There is no decision that we did not make jointly over the years. Through both the good times and the tough times, she has always answered the bell. However, it was during the tough times that she was at her best. Nobody is better. Nobody. She will continue to lead you to even greater heights. I am sure of it.

The leadership level at BMI is extraordinary, and the cupboard is overflowing with talent and then some. Because I came up from the ranks, and had performed every job each of you now do, is probably the reason I respect and admire every one of you so much. I know how hard it is to do every day, again and again and again.

Why would I leave now? We reached our apex in billings in 2000, before some of you were even here. However, all of us knew that if we looked too hard, there were a good number of "one account wonders" who were making placements, but frankly, didn't really know what they were doing. 2001-2004 were brutal in every respect a company can experience. However, just as fire tempers steel, that time made many of you into the extraordinary talents you are today. We became a better company. Those of you who were here know we were aggressive, and new ideas and *procedures were happening all of the time. Some things worked and some didn't, but we landed on it instead of it landing on us. We have now returned to the Super Bowl. Our billings/recruiter is 50 percent higher than in 2000. We now have multiple $400-500K billers, and $100K in a quarter is considered good, but not extraordinary. I leave with BMI on top, and to be honest that is a fulfilling feeling.*

I will miss seeing or talking to you on a daily basis. I have spent many hours with each of you, and I hope that when the time came for me to deliver the goods for you, that I did.

Most of those things I once did personally have been delegated over the years. I look around and know that I have not been guilty of the entrepreneur's worst sin – that he and only he can do it. The talent that surrounds me is unbelievable, but you already know that.

One of the things I have great confidence in is my ability to make really big decisions well; where to go to college, who to marry, whether to leave the Navy, and the decision to enter our world. And now the decision to leave BMI. This is right for me and for my family. And for you.

Of all the things I hope you think of when you think of me, and I hope lives on well after I'm gone, are the values I tried to live each day, and I know are in the DNA of BMI.

It's not the placements or the procedures or the systems that make BMI a magical place. It is each of you, and your relationships with each other. When I think of each of you in the future, I will not think of how much you billed. No, I will think of a funny story or a good time we shared.

I have always believed that a leader should feel he has to earn, on a daily basis, the right to lead high-speed people. As I leave, I hope you feel I earned that right with you. It has truly been an honor.

Shaun

So I sold, retired, resigned; whatever you want to call it. A lot of people dream of retiring at 50. I was 51, but retiring at that age was never my goal. It just sort of happened. We had dug ourselves out of the 2001-2004 recession. Our placements and sales actually exceeded 2000, which had been our previous peak year, and I came up for air. I had always been so focused on my responsibilities to my family, to the company, and to my people that I never really thought about what I wanted or needed. I know that sounds hard to believe, but it's true. I enjoyed the company and loved the work, but I had not previously thought about myself.

I looked around and thought maybe now was the time. I could never leave when things were bad, but they looked good and promised to be good for the foreseeable future. (Little did I or anybody else know what was looming.) All of my senior people had between 10-14 years with BMI, and they were good, really good, and Sandy wanted to stay, so I could just sell to her and not have to deal with selling to an outsider. I also knew that eventually things would turn south again, as they always do, and I would never leave until things got better and I could be in my 60's by then.

I also think I was tired. While I still loved my people and the business, the conflicts that are inherent in even a successful partnership build up over time, especially one that had lasted more than 16 years. There was also no doubt the 2001-2004 recession had taken its toll on me. Now was the time. It felt right.

As I ventured into retirement, I found reactions to me curious. Some people were glad for me, some were jealous of me, and some wanted to be me. I was a young man to have been able to do what I did. I found I did not miss the inherent stream of little issues that go with running a business. I certainly did not miss knowing that if things went badly I could be wiped out. What I did miss was being a person of influence with my people. I was a father figure to many of them, and I liked that role.

I had been involved in coaching youth sport teams for many years and that world proved crucial to me as I left BMI. It provided me with a passion and great camaraderie and a mission that mattered. A lot of people thought I retired to be able to spend more time with my family, which really wasn't the case. I was fortunate and had already spent that time and did not feel the need to change anything. In fact, I told people the only way I could spend more time with my kids would be to enroll in their school, and sit in the desk next to them.

I made a couple of decisions that I think helped. I decided I wasn't going to be anything but supportive of BMI and any changes that were made. My standard line was, "If I was Sandy and was replacing me, I would make changes, too." Obviously people were trolling me for my opinion on any changes with which they thought I might not agree. I didn't give them the chance. There were also comments by people missing some of the things I did or how I did them. I told them, if there was something I had done that they liked, it was now time for them to do it themselves.

In addition, since my payout from BMI was dependent on the company doing well, I had a vested interest in things continuing in a positive direction. However, I didn't worry too much about that, because I knew BMI was in great shape. Six months later, the economy imploded, and a lot of things were about to change. While I would still get a minimum payment from BMI, much of my payout was based on how the company was doing, and if it didn't generate a certain amount then some of the payout could be delayed. As time went on, this resulted in a new payout being negotiated, which helped BMI get through the tough times. Besides, a bankrupt BMI wasn't going to be able to pay me anything anyway. In the end, a private equity group purchased more than 50 percent of BMI and I was paid what I was owed. A happy ending for all.

Shaun G. Bradley

CHAPTER 2

My Beginning in Recruiting

I left the Navy in April, 1987, after completing my last tour as the Aviation Supply Officer onboard the nuclear aircraft carrier USS CARL VINSON (CVN-70). Having responsibility for 100+ sailors and officers changes a person, and I know it did me. Much of the leadership success I later enjoyed, I owe to what I learned from my then boss, Commander (later Rear Admiral) Mitchell, and my Leading Chief Petty Officer, Master Chief Mike Griffith.

I returned home to Green Bay, Wisconsin, to spend time with my mom, who had been sick for many years and to figure out my next step. I also transferred into the Navy Reserves, which was a good decision. I was able to be promoted to Lieutenant Commander (O-4) with my year group peers and also earn some walking-around money, which didn't hurt.

With a Naval Academy degree, along with a Master's Degree in hand, I thought I would somehow be marketable, but wasn't sure. When you grow up in a blue-collar factory town, and go straight from high school to a service academy to the Navy, your familiarity with Corporate America is pretty limited. As one of my areas of responsibility while in the Navy was to supervise the flight deck forklift drivers, I even made sure I had my own forklift driver's license in case I ever needed one to get a job. I really didn't know what awaited me in the civilian world. I would learn in my military recruiting career just how common this sentiment was among veterans entering the civilian workforce.

My Master's Degree was in Educational Leadership from Western Michigan University. While home in Green Bay, I investigated a career in education, and knew a local principal who was interested in helping me pursue one. However, I soon learned that for me to become an elementary school teacher (I was interested in being a principal and coach down the road), I would have to go back to college for three additional years. After graduation, I would then make less than half of what I was making when I left the Navy. I wasn't willing to sacrifice three years for that kind of money. I was actually interviewed by U.S. News & World Report as a person the education world was missing out on, because my qualifications did not fit squarely into the education establishment requirements. This was before there were programs like Troops to Teachers and the like to get people with business and industry experience into teaching. So, I moved on. I could scratch the coaching itch in other ways, which I eventually would do.

I went to a local resume guy in Green Bay, who really saw me coming. He put together a resume that was on all four pages of a glorified manila folder. When I mentioned to him that I thought resumes were supposed to only be one-page long, he shot back, "Do you do resumes for a living or do I?" So off I went with probably the worst looking resume ever.

I sent my "stellar" resume to the military recruiting firms of the day, which were listed in the classified section of Navy Times and got a great response from a recruiter at Fox-Morris in Philadelphia. I had a bunch of really good interviews with companies like Polaroid, KPMG, Abbott Labs, Pepsi, Johnson & Johnson, and others. To demonstrate how clueless I was about Corporate America, when the recruiter briefed me on one of my first interviews, he told me it was with a Fortune 500 Company. My response was, "What's a Fortune 500 Company?" Remember my background.

The other firms never called me or called me a lot later than the Fox-Morris recruiter had. Whether I was a good candidate or not, my profile was in the sweet spot of what the military recruiting industry was placing.

When the time came for me to start my recruiting career, I assumed there were a lot of candidates similar to me, who the other firms were neglecting. I never forgot that lesson and when I began recruiting, I always called a new candidate the first time chance I had. I would be first and ahead of my competition.

However, looking back, I know I wanted something different. I had even taken out an ad for myself in USA Today, which read, "Academy grad looking for an opportunity," and received some nibbles. I was not averse to sales and, in particular, commission sales. A lot of people steer clear of that world, but I wanted to be paid for what I did. I had fond memories while growing up as the top boy selling bags of peanuts at Lambeau Field. I was selling 600 bags of peanuts a game and #2 was selling 400. Believe me, 600 bags of peanuts is a lot of peanuts.

All of these things came together when I received a call from the last military recruiting company, The Lucas Group (TLG), to contact me. I had already started to wonder about all of the jobs into which the recruiters were trying to place me. If those jobs were so great, why weren't they doing them? I thought what they were doing must be better. (I actually used this line many times in future years to recruit my own people for BMI.) This led to interviews and an offer to help start the military recruiting operation in Atlanta for TLG.

Prior to arriving in Atlanta, I received fashion tips from a men's store in Green Bay, which convinced me that, along with a couple of suits and ties, I should have at least five long-sleeve AND five short-sleeve dress shirts depending on the occasion. Inexperienced didn't even begin to describe me. So off I went to Atlanta. On my first day, there was an off-site training event, with everybody in the company there, having just returned from a company trip to the Cayman Islands. They were all dressed in shorts and flip-flops, and here I was in my new suit and vest, looking seriously out of place. My welcome also involved a woman telling me that no one at TLG had ever made any money doing military recruiting. Not an auspicious start, but the day did have a highlight. Another young gal, who I guess felt sorry for me, sat with me at lunch. She would eventually become my wife.

The next day, my future partner, Sandy, let the training, which was quite good. I was being taught how to take control of an interview. About two hours into training, my new boss came in and said, "What are you doing? You don't have time for training. We have interviews scheduled in four weeks, and you need to get some candidates."

With zero recruiting experience, and fresh out of the military, I began. The Atlanta military operation had been defunct for two years, so we were starting from scratch. However, I knew this could be a great opportunity and my attitude was that I had seven days in a week and 24 hours in a day and I would use them as needed. For my first two years, I worked every day, including every weekend.

The military has a natural number of people who leave the service every month. When I started, many of them were already committed to working with the other military recruiting firms, which were our competition. However, I knew many of the future candidates were not signed up and most of the firms were just not that aggressive. I decided to live for today as best I could, and target those who would be leaving the service in 6-12 months. I would then spend time with them and build relationships before the other firms had them in their sights. This enabled me to leap ahead of my competitors, many of whom had years in the industry.

When I entered the industry in 1987, the military recruiting business was very small and consisted of pretty much Mom and Pop operations. In 1987, as the first military hire for TLG in Atlanta, we made just four placements. In 1988, I was the first recruiter in company history to bill over $200K in a year and based on our success, TLG expanded its military operation. I was named VP/GM shortly thereafter. In 1990, we placed 400 people and were responsible for 90 percent of the company's profits.

We assembled an unbelievable collection of talent. Together during that unique period of time, were the future founders or those who formed the leadership core of the three military recruiting firms that would dominate the industry for the next 25 years (BMI, TLG and Orion). All of them were either my candidates or my hires. (I always did have an eye for talent.)

I left TLG in early1991, which surprised a lot of people. Frankly, I wasn't happy. While our success there was phenomenal and our growth meteoric, not everybody handles that kind of success well. Some were among the best people I've ever known, but others weren't. Assembling an all-star team is tricky business. Some major producers thought they were the very reason for the team's success, not the other way around. I learned valuable lessons on how to put together a team of the kind of people I wanted to spend my future with. I would be more careful next time.

I was 35 years old, with $100,000 in the bank, and a young man's energy. I was married, with a seven-month-old daughter at home. My wife had left TLG the previous year and was supportive. I had options. I also knew there was a window where I had cash, and my family situation could absorb risk. I knew that window would not last forever. I was at a point in my life where I wanted to do my own thing. I just wasn't sure what my own thing was. I had always been friends with Sandy Morris, and about a month after I left TLG, we had lunch and talked about going into business together.

Sandy and I launched our company in July 1991 and moved into a 250-square-foot executive suite. Our corporate office was in Atlanta and we would open additional offices in San Diego, Austin, Norfolk, and Chicago, which would swell our ranks to well over 100 people. We would eventually place more than 15,000 veterans into industry, and be honored in the White House as one of the top small businesses in the country. Our annual sales would exceed $15M, and we would be in the top 1 percent of all non-franchised staffing firms in the U.S.

While our accomplishments were significant, what motivated me, as much or more than the money, was the knowledge that my people were doing great. Many bought nice houses and their spouses were happy with what they were doing. I felt they had bet on me and that bet had turned out well for them. I can remember the first time I met many of the spouses, in particular, the wives. Initially, I would almost always get the look that said, "So, you're the guy who convinced my husband to do this." Then, later on, the wives would be effusive in their praise. They often told me, "He loves what he does and he loves the company." Words like that always made me feel good.

I remember in the early days being scared out of my mind. I had left a job where I made $232,000 the previous year, but now I was staring at having no income for the foreseeable future. My CPA asked me if I had lost my mind. I frequently asked myself late at night,"What did I do? What did I do? What did I do?" I remember coming home from a movie on a Saturday night and getting ready to go into work. My wife asked me where I was going. I told her, "To work." She asked, "Why are you doing that?" I told her, "I can stay in bed and not sleep, or I can go into the office. Maybe I won't get anything done, but I can't just sit here and not try to affect things."

We didn't take out any loans to start the company, because it never dawned on us that anybody would consider loaning "us" money. It was a good decision at the time, but it nonetheless made for a hard road with us not getting paychecks for the first 16 months of the company's existence. Sandy ran the money and she would ask me, "Do you want the good news or the bad?" I would tell her that I wanted the good news. Her response, "The good news is you're not getting a paycheck." I would then ask her for the bad news. She would then often say, "You need to write a check to the company for $10,000, so we can pay our bills." I would eventually bounce five personal checks, and Sandy would make payroll on her credit card before it turned. Paying for things ourselves became a mindset, and we funded our expansions out of hide by having one successful office, and then multiple successful offices, pay for the additional operations we launched.

About a year into our business, we were on fumes. I had gone through most of the $100,000 I had started with, and while I could see things were going in the right direction, that still didn't pay the bills. People can say what they want about Wal-Mart, but in many respects, they saved BMI. Sandy was able to convince them to give us an opportunity to place store managers. When they showed up, they brought along a company drug tester, and were going to make offers on the spot, which was a very rare occurrence. They ended up making 16 offers and we placed 11. While the start dates for most of our candidates were a few months out, and we had to wait for the money, we knew it was coming. Every day we waited for the check to arrive. Anybody who knew us was aware we were waiting on that money. "Has it come in yet?" was always asked. When it came, we finally breathed, and a copy of that check was framed and had a place of honor in our office for many years.

Afterwards, I sent a letter to Wal-Mart about the difference they had made in helping us make it. This was around the same time the Alan Jackson song, "The Little Man," came out. That song was a thinly disguised slam on Wal-Mart. It told the story of the big company coming to town and destroying the small businesses that had previously been there. I thought we made for a good story about how Wal-Mart actually helped to save a small company.

The staffing industry is all about people, but even within that industry, the military recruiting business is unique. Our specialty was placing veterans as they left the service at no cost to the veteran. We were a contingency staffing firm. This means if a company gave us a job order and our candidate was hired, we would be paid a fee. If, in the end, our candidate was not hired, we wouldn't be paid anything, regardless of the amount of work we had done. It was pure pay-for-performance.

Our methods of making this happen were twofold. The first was via a Hiring Conference (HC). These were held in a suite hotel on a Sunday and Monday, and were where companies could interview eight to ten already screened candidates in a single day. Follow-up interviews at the company's site were then scheduled, when there was mutual interest. The HC took place on Sunday and Monday because it was simply easier for the military candidates to take a three-day weekend than it was for them to get time off in the middle of the week. The second method was by setting up initial interviews that occurred by telephone or in person, independent of an HC. We called these Off-Conference (OC) interviews.

The jobs our people did were pretty straightforward. Candidate Recruiters (CRs) were always military veterans and, as the name suggests, were responsible for bringing qualified candidates into our program that were considering leaving the service. Account Representatives (ARs) were responsible for establishing and managing relationships with hiring managers that led to BMI being given assignments to fill their job openings. About half of the ARs were ex-military and half were civilians. We also had Conference Coordinators (CCs) who were responsible for all facets of running our HCs. This was a promotable and very demanding position. Most were initially CRs. This position entailed scheduling as many as 600+ individual interviews in a single day, for as many as 70 companies and more than 130 candidates. Each had their own schedule and preferences. The most HCs any CC would run during a year would be eight to ten. As time went on, and we became more successful, we would run nearly 100 HCs nationally, in various locations around the country. We held them every weekend of the year except for the major holidays

We paid our people on a draw (advance pay), which would be paid back in future commissions. The draw could vary depending on background and personal needs. As somebody who liked commission sales, I wanted to hire people who felt the same way. I wanted all of us to be able to make money together, and didn't mind sharing. However, if things got rough, I also wanted everyone to be in the same boat, feeling some anxiety and pulling hard to get where we needed to be. I would tell people during the interview process that BMI was not the place to come to get motivated. It was the place to come and be rewarded for already being that way.

What came to pass was a national company of commission sales people working together. Many of these people were high performers with unique personalities. Many placements had as many as six people getting a piece of the fee for making different parts of the placements happen. When I describe it to people, they can hardly believe it because few things are more individualized than commission sales. To make that function at a high level within a team framework is pretty difficult.

During our formative years, we focused exclusively on manufacturing and technical leadership positions, and only filled positions in locations east of the Mississippi River. Our candidates were Commissioned Officers with a technical background. The target group, and the most easily identified, were service academy graduates who all had technical degrees and the leadership experience gained while in the military. While 25 percent of our placements were with service academy graduates, there were many graduates of other schools who were commissioned through Reserve Officer Training Corps (ROTC) programs and fit the bill. However, the name recognition of West Point and Annapolis helped us to sell the concept of hiring military people to our clients. We would eventually move into placing Enlisted candidates with a technical background. This area would eclipse Officer placements in both number and revenue. IT/Telecom and Medical would also be added and down the road we would establish an operation placing candidates into Sales positions, as well.

We placed the same types of candidates over and over into the same types of positions over and over, although there were certainly differences in company locations, industries and salaries. The candidates also had their own particular needs and desires. However, there were enough similarities on each side to enable us to industrialize the entire recruiting process. The standard operating procedure in most recruiting firms was to receive an assignment from a client to fill a job opening, and then "search" to find a candidate who met the position specifications. We didn't have to "search" for our candidates. We already had them in our program, and we had them in volume. It was our speed in being able to fill client job orders, and our ultra-focus on placing specific types of candidates into a well-defined group of positions, that made this possible.

The best comparison to our type of recruiting would probably be major college football recruiting. We typically knew where our candidates could be found. Then it was up to us to establish relationships with them, see if they were a fit, and recruit them to work with us. And just as colleges establish relationships with great prospects early, so did we. We knew the types of positions our clients were looking to fill, and we focused our efforts accordingly. The biggest difference was a college football recruiting staff was recruiting for just one school. BMI had clients numbering in excess of a thousand.

We were not dependent on any one-industry segment to be successful, which was a huge advantage. Our candidates were unbelievably talented, and the types of people any industry would want. We placed them into virtually every business sector from manufacturing to service, from high-tech to low-tech, from finance to telecommunications, and from the automotive industry to mobile home manufacturing. We placed them in the largest metro areas and in small towns in the middle of nowhere. We placed them into multi-national conglomerates with hundreds of thousands of employees and with tiny companies of fewer than 10. We placed them into everything and everywhere. As long as some segments of the economy were doing OK, then so were we.

CHAPTER 3

The Placement Machine

BMI developed a set of processes, systems, and interlocking steps that helped us make our placements. We called it The Placement Machine. And just like any machine, it required constant tweaking and was only as good as the people running it. The essential parts of this entire process were having the right BMI people, high quality candidates and corporate clients who were interested in hiring them. I will discuss each of these in the chapters ahead, but, for now, I want to describe The Placement Machine, as it provides an overview on how we did it.

As it is impossible to describe our operation without utilizing some of our own internal language, I used acronyms (AR, CR, CC and HC) in both this chapter and throughout the book, for both brevity and to minimize the tediousness of reading the same words over and over again. I have included a Glossary of Terms which I hope helps.

For some readers, the level of detail in this chapter will seem like overkill. For others, it will read like a recipe book on how to start and run a military recruiting firm. As with many major undertakings, it might seem easier than it really was. Regardless, understanding how we did what we did provides background I hope will place the following chapters in perspective.

Much of our system could be favorably compared to how a distribution or fulfillment center operates (with a dating-service flavor thrown in to make it interesting). We put the right candidates in front of the right companies, arranged for them to meet, and, hopefully, like each other. We had a large number of clients, as well as candidates, and they were pretty well aligned as to what each side was looking for. The real trick was to know each client and each candidate well enough to make the right potential matches, increasing the odds that once they met each other, they would, in fact, go the distance to job offer and acceptance.

Once we had a candidate in our program, we developed a structured program to ensure that candidate would be ready to interview with our client companies. These steps included the following elements:

Candidate Prep

Our candidate preparation was extensive and included interviewing advice, resume review and guidance (no four-pagers!), direction on what to wear to an interview, suggested books to read prior to the interview, and an inspection of each candidate's paperwork. We also had multiple conversations to educate and answer questions on what awaited candidates as they started to interview, as well as once they began their civilian careers.

One of our most important tasks was to shepherd them through this journey, so they were their best selves when they interviewed. Frankly, these candidates were great, and we knew both from meeting them and understanding their military performance evaluations just how good they were. However, confidence is crucial when interviewing, and our job was to help them be confident and enthusiastic during theirs. Fear of the unknown is present in every single person leaving the service. (It certainly was for me.) Consequently, all of our efforts in preparing our candidates were geared towards decreasing their anxiety level.

Interviewing Advice

Practicing answers to commonly asked questions helps, but our best advice to candidates was to study themselves. We reminded them that if they were studying for an exam, they would study the course materials. In this instance, their life was the textbook, and we advised them to review their entire life from the beginning. This included where they lived, what their parents did, where they went to elementary school, and who their friends were, going all the way back to their earliest memories. This was not because they would be asked questions about where they went to grade school, but because it would help them shake the cobwebs loose in their brain about their entire life, and better prepare them to answer all types of questions.

We gave them specific guidance, the most important being: never talk for longer than two minutes - NEVER. Nobody wants to listen to a rambler. We told them to have numbers and details ready to place any point they were making into perspective for the interviewer. As they were interviewing for leadership positions, using the word "we" in any answer was a lot more important than using "I." We advised them to not only be ready with questions about the opportunity, but to also ask the interviewers about themselves. Everyone likes to talk about themselves. The goal of every interview is to make it into a conversation – get the interviewer to like them.

We told them their mindset and attitude should be similar to when they met the parents of their boyfriend or girlfriend for the first time. Be formal, but not too formal; be friendly, but not too much. We told them a firm handshake and a smile when they met the interviewer went a long way. We also showed them how body language, such as leaning forward in their chair when they spoke, showed interest and enthusiasm, while slouching back was fatal to their chances.

Resume

The candidate's resume was crucial. There is a difference of opinion on how a military resume should be structured. Some say to eliminate all acronyms and military terminology and totally civilianize it. Having seen some of these resumes, where even I was unable to understand what the candidate had done, I don't agree. Those resumes can perhaps better navigate a key word search program, but fall short in providing a picture of what the candidate actually did. Acronyms and military jargon, along with anything that would obviously be foreign to a person with no military background should be eliminated, but basic military terms can be used to explain the candidate's experience. A platoon is a platoon is a platoon and a tank is a tank is a tank.

One of the things that helped us was sending sample resumes to candidates well in advance of when they would write their resume. We included an explanation of each area, and why the resume should be prepared our way. As with most things, it was a lot easier to have the end product be high quality if the base product was good from the beginning.

Recommended Reading List

We provided a list of 10 books on interviewing tips, career guidance and general business overviews for each candidate to read. This familiarized them to some degree with the business world, possibly giving them some ideas as to what they might want to do. More importantly, it let them know the civilian business world was not as foreign and different as they might have initially thought it would be.

Candidate Relationship

The CR was the point person responsible for managing and developing our relationship with each candidate. This involved answering their questions, educating them on the different types of positions and industries available to them, and providing resume guidance. Most important of all was to learn their story. Knowing their personal situation was crucial to not only having accurate and timely information on each candidate, but also in establishing a level of trust, which helped to facilitate the relationship. The smart candidates initiated a relationship with a military recruiting firm well before the date they could leave the service. Some eventually stayed in the service, but when they did, it was because they had made an informed and positive decision to do so.

Candidates often asked us what they could do to help improve their civilian world marketability. Our advice was to continue to do well in the military. Sometimes people would earn master's degrees, as I did and think that was going to be their ticket to landing a great civilian position. Certainly getting an advanced degree can never be a bad thing, but I saw a major disconnect between what candidates thought a master's degree would do for them and what it actually did. I never saw, not once, a client hire any of our candidates where a master's degree was the deciding factor.

Our Enlisted Technician candidates had extraordinary qualifications. Regardless of their technical field, they had all received extensive academic training in their particular area from military schools. What made this training unique was the military only sends the "cream" as instructors at these schools. Hence, they were trained by the best. This was combined with the actual hands-on experience they gained while in their units. Unfortunately, their military experience didn't always translate into the civilian world's licensing requirements. The military could have helped a lot more by ensuring they received civilian licenses while on active duty, since in many cases, they were essentially doing the same work as their civilian counterparts.

Pre-Hiring Conference

Six months from the candidate's projected availability date, we planned which HC the candidate should attend. A formal invitation was sent out at 90 days, and interviews took place at 60 days. These dates were flexible, but that was the ideal. Clients understood they had to wait for candidates to transition out of the service before they could start work, but they didn't want to wait too long. They had needs, too, and wanted their job openings filled as soon as possible. This timeframe then placed the candidates in the interviewing window where their CR would begin to look at opportunities for them.

Candidate Hiring Conference Invitation

This was an incredibly important document. This officially and formally invited the candidates to the HC, and our expectation was they would attend. This invitation laid out all of the logistics, including where and when the HC would take place, and provided detailed instructions on making hotel reservations and when to arrive, as well as when to depart. A reminder on what was needed to complete the candidate file was also included.

Interviewing Attire for Candidates

This was more complicated than one might imagine. Military people wear a uniform to work every day and while some might understand what business wear is, many did not. Consequently, we were very specific and detailed on what to wear for both men and women. These detailed instructions were also communicated in our HC invitations. Interviewing attire for men was navy blue or charcoal gray suit, white oxford or similar dress shirt, burgundy or red pattern tie, and dress shoes with matching belt and socks. Reminders about not wearing unit insignias and other eye-catching things were also sent.

Similar guidance was provided to female candidates, with specific instructions on skirt length, make-up, flashy jewelry, and high heels. The goal was for the candidates to be the focus of the interviewer, not what they were wearing. There were no points added for wearing something good; only points taken away for wearing something inappropriate, or that stood out. Not all of the candidates would listen to our directions, and if candidates wouldn't listen to us on what to wear, they certainly weren't going to listen to us on where to go to work. (I never placed a male candidate who wore a yellow tie.)

We learned this lesson the hard way, prior to providing specific guidance in writing on what to wear to the HC interviews. I had a candidate who was an absolute blue-chipper. He was a Naval Academy graduate and African-American Navy pilot who looked like a million bucks. Prior to the HC, I reminded him that he needed to wear a navy blue suit to his interviews. Well, he showed up on Monday wearing his Navy uniform with pilot wings, medals, the whole nine yards. I asked him where his suit was. He said, "I'm wearing it. You told me to wear a navy blue suit – I thought you meant this." Of course, he went 10 for 10 at the HC. Every company wanted him. He was so good he could have worn pajamas to his interviews. Not every candidate could have gotten away with that.

We had another candidate show up for Monday's interviews wearing a god-awful blue shirt that was not going to cut it with our clients. He was roughly the same size and body build as my good friend and co-worker,

Eric Stagliano, USNA '81, who was wearing a nice, crisp white dress shirt. I told Eric that he needed to take one for the team and switch shirts with him, which Eric agreed to do. Unfortunately, this guy had a perspiration issue and had sweated through the armpits of his shirt. After the HC, Eric came to me and said, "Shaun, I'll pretty much do anything for you, but I'll never do that again." We learned to be specific in providing guidance on what to wear and to do it in writing.

Haircut at Airport

We had a candidate come to the HC who had tremendous credentials – Navy Nuclear Trained Officer (Nuke), with a degree in Mechanical Engineering from Cal Tech. He had been out of the service for about six months and had let his hair grow, and I mean grow. It wasn't in a ponytail, but it was really long. Remember, he was interviewing amidst a group of military officers with military haircuts. After introductions, I told him he needed to go get a haircut. This was in the morning at about 10 a.m. I'm thinking he can just scoot out, get a haircut, and come right back. As Sunday was the day for interview preparation, logistics and company briefs, it was important that he be there to get that information. At 5 p.m., he strolled back into the hotel, and I asked him where he had been. He said he had to drive all the way to the Atlanta Airport to get a haircut, as all of the barbershops in Atlanta were closed on Sunday. Unbelievable. From then on I was a lot more careful on what I told candidates to do.

Baton Principle

In a big operation like ours, it was really important for one person to have positive control of a candidate at all times, as it was too easy for candidates to slip through the cracks. Hence, we established a baton principle similar to a track relay team. The CR had responsibility for the candidate pre-HC, and the CC had control at and immediately after the HC. If the candidate wasn't placed, the baton was then passed back to the original CR to look for new employment opportunities for the candidate.

Hiring Conference

The central vehicle for making placements was the HC. This was where the companies would come to interview a pre-selected slate of candidates, and the candidates would have a lineup of companies that met their needs and desires. This was totally unlike a job fair, where the company representatives stand behind a table and the candidates walk up with a resume in hand and speak to them for a minute, hoping to both learn about the company and generate enough interest to garner an interview.

Even with us controlling and scheduling every interview, this process could still be very messy. There were very few times that the clients and candidates had perfect fits for their entire line-ups. Military candidates typically weren't sure what they really wanted to do and were learning as they went through the process. What they were looking for easily changed along the way. Companies were often learning about the military and military candidates as well, and it often evolved on their end, when they saw a fit only after they understood what the candidate had actually done. Many times our clients would interview candidates and see them as fits for openings in their company that we didn't even know about. Historically, 95 percent of the candidates who attended an HC had at least one company they interviewed with show interest in them, and the companies typically liked 60 percent of the candidates they interviewed.

Critical Mass

Perhaps the hardest thing to do in the military recruiting world is to create the critical mass necessary to even put on an HC. The companies need to see a slate of qualified candidates and the candidates want to have interviews with companies that interest them. There are a lot of different types of companies as well as candidates, so it wasn't only the challenge of convincing companies and candidates it was worth their time and money to attend; it was the additional challenge of ensuring the right candidates and companies came, so that one side of the ledger was well matched with the other.

How do you get enough companies to convince the right candidates to attend an HC and vice versa? It truly is a chicken-and-egg scenario, and getting both companies and candidates to travel on their own dime, especially in the beginning when you have no history with either, is incredibly difficult. This is one of the primary reasons why every successful military recruiting firm had at least two (often more) founders to focus on ensuring each side of the equation was successful. When BMI started, Sandy focused on selling the clients and I focused on recruiting the candidates and running the HCs.

Hiring Conference Scheduling

For many years, putting the HC schedule together had been done manually with multiple grids on long sheets of paper. Some interviews were 30 minutes long, some were 45, and some were for an hour. The HC interviews started at 8 a.m. and finished at 5 p.m., but some clients showed up after 8 a.m. and/or had to leave early. Some were there for half a day. An hour lunch typically started at noon, but not for all. We could have made our interview schedule more structured and defined, but we tried to accommodate our clients' particular needs as best we could.

However, as we became more successful, the number of clients and candidates who participated in our HCs increased, which served to make the HC interview puzzle even more complex. We tried to find scheduling software to help, but none was flexible enough for us. We were told by some programmers that what we needed for our schedule was not possible; there were simply too many variables. Eventually, we got it done and our scheduling software problem was solved. The standardization and automation enabled us to conduct HCs nationally and on a massive scale. It worked well, and what had previously taken 20-30 man-hours to create and check, double check and then triple check, was typically completed in under five hours.

Hiring Conference Sunday/Monday

Sunday was Prep Day. All of the candidates were required to check in by 9 a.m. and provide us with any missing information for their file. Next came the introductions between our staff and the candidates in the ballroom of the hotel. All of the candidates would stand, introduce themselves, and provide brief information about their background. A lot of them knew each other and had either gone to school or had served together, so the camaraderie and energy of the group were always fun to experience. Then came the interview preparation where candidates were reminded of the interviewing skills we had discussed prior to the HC. Next, each individual candidate's schedule was given to the attendees. As every schedule was customized for each one, no two schedules were the same.

Every company that was interviewing would then be briefed by the responsible AR. Each was on a 15 minute clock. A written and oral brief, along with company literature, were provided to each candidate describing the company, location, position, interviewer's name and background, along with specific or unique information on that company. There was also an opportunity to ask questions, and since my people were at the HC all day, questions and discussion of the opportunity frequently took place even after the brief was completed. Clients often had particular wants or needs, and not every candidate was able to interview with every company they wanted to see. This situation required deft handling in explaining to candidates why they were not interviewing with a particular company. The day would typically finish in the evening, depending on how many clients were at the HC. A full and exhausting day!

During that afternoon and evening, our clients would typically check into the hotel unless they were local. They would let us know they had arrived, and would want to see their schedule of candidates to interview, along with their resumes. We would frequently get pushback from the clients on why certain candidates were in their lineup, as maybe they didn't exactly fit the position requirements. We would then have to advocate for those candidates and explain why we felt the client should talk to them. The number of placements that came from us doing this was countless. Typically, even the best resume, and in particular a military resume, just doesn't provide the entire picture. We often would tell the client to hold us accountable and trust us. This is one of the reasons why, time after time, the candidates we put in front of companies without the "stated" requirements ended up getting the job. We knew the company would like them and create flexibility in the position requirements to get them onboard. In addition, the advertised position was often not the only one the company had to fill. By having candidates who might be highly qualified, but not interested in that particular position or location, still interview with the company, we knew they had an excellent chance of landing the right position.

Monday was interview day. The candidates would show up at 7:30 a.m. and interviews started at 8 a.m. Prior to this, we would have breakfast with clients who had checked in on Sunday, or meet with local clients who were arriving to give them their client packet. Interviews would occur throughout the day, and there were countless little things to deal with. Typical issues included a candidate going to the wrong room, a client keeping candidates too long, so they were late for their next interview, clients telling us they had new requirements and wanted to see additional or different candidates, candidates not showing up for an interview because they decided they weren't interested in the location, and on and on. The only thing that saved us, as we had hundreds of interviews going on, was to have the pre-HC plan so wired that we could focus on the exceptions. Running an HC took serious leadership and communication skills and a cool head. Our CCs were special people.

At the end of the day, every candidate checked out with us prior to leaving. They also filled out an essential document that provided us with all of the key information we needed for their follow-up interviews. This included their current and future contact info, their schedule over the next month, including days they could not interview, the earliest date they could start work, a preliminary ranking of the companies that interviewed them, and their interest level in those companies. They were then given a time to call us on Tuesday morning to learn the companies' feedback on them. Simultaneously, the clients were checking out and providing us with their feedback on the candidates. They might also tell us where and when they wanted to do follow-up interviews, and how those interviews would take place.

Post- Hiring Conference Feedback

By now we had reviewed the client feedback, knew the client interest level in each candidate and the results of every interview. When the candidates called in at their pre-scheduled time, we provided them with their feedback and put together a game plan for follow-up interviews. Giving feedback to each candidate took real skill. We had to find out their true desires, and not waste time with follow-up interviews for positions where they would never take the offer. It was in their best interest as well as the clients' for the candidates to only pursue opportunities where there was true interest. If the candidates weren't interested in the companies that had interviewed them, we certainly were big enough to find something they would like.

There was also some ego management that occurred during these calls. If particular candidates had aced the HC, and most of the companies they had interviewed with liked them, but we felt they were a little too "big for their britches," we discussed with them, at length, the companies that did not want to pursue them. This may seem harsh, but as we spent a lot more time with the candidates than the interviewers did, we knew that if those candidates didn't take it down a notch, it would cause them problems when the clients did spend the time. In the end, no matter how great the credentials, they still had to like the candidate. During my early years in recruiting, I sent a candidate on an interview who had unbelievable credentials. Incredible really. The feedback from the client was that he had the best background of anyone they had ever interviewed, but they didn't want any part of him. They couldn't stand him.

On the other hand, if we had a candidate who didn't do as well as expected, we really tried, while still providing constructive feedback, to emphasize the companies that were interested, while providing reassurance that we were still confident in their future success. Candidates, regardless of their background, are very vulnerable during this process, and it is important a recruiter realizes it. Remembering what it was like when we left the military, and went through the interviewing process helped. This is the time when a recruiter can really help somebody or really do damage.

We then spoke to our clients about the candidates they liked, and who we recommended for second interviews. This also required a deft touch, as sometimes clients wanted to pursue candidates regardless of our recommendations. Often they felt they had made a connection with the candidate, and were stunned when the candidate wasn't interested in them.

Post-Hiring Conference Guidance to Clients

We did our best to educate our clients, both before and after the HC, on the best way to get the candidates they wanted by providing guidance on proven practices that yielded results. We emphasized how a lack of speed is perceived by candidates as a lack of interest, and as they were in a competitive situation, they would lose on the candidates they wanted if they moved too slowly. We also had some clients who just didn't get it when it came to recruiting or interviewing people. Many interviewers feel it is up to the candidates to sell them on why they should be hired. While this is true, it is also the responsibility of the interviewer to sell the candidates on the opportunity. I suppose if you are the company EVERY candidate wants to work for, you can get away with that, but for most companies getting great people requires a little more. It normally takes about five minutes into an interview (if that) to figure out if you like the candidate or not. At that point, the interviewer should shift gears and start to woo the candidate and establish a relationship. This is just not that hard. A candidate wants to feel the love. The recruiting process is akin to dating; responsiveness and positive feedback are crucial parts.

The hiring process of many companies is slow and plodding, and requires a bureaucracy to get approval. It's almost as if the more people who are involved in hiring, the less accountability there is for anybody to be held responsible for a mistake. The candidate perceives speed as love, and the faster you move, the better the likelihood the candidate will feel truly wanted. Speed is all-important when it comes to getting the people you want.

Post-Hiring Conference Guidance to Candidates

We sent additional and comprehensive information to each candidate on what to expect after the HC and how this phase of their career search would work. We told them to have a packet prepared, and to carry it with them on every follow-up interview. This packet needed to include college transcripts, copies of their military performance evaluations, a list of references with their contact information, and extra copies of their resume. They could be asked for any of this information, and having it immediately available would make a positive impression. Just like we did at the HC, we told them to have thank you notes ready to be filled out and mailed to every person they had spoken to before leaving the city to return home.

Hotel

The relationship with our HC hotel was crucial. When we opened in 1991, I met with the Sales Manager at the Atlanta Sheraton-Galleria, and told her what we wanted to do. They were the perfect size for us, with plenty of meeting space and hotel rooms. Most importantly, our HC would be the largest and most important event going on at the hotel over the weekend. We would be the show.

Unkown to us at the time we selected Sunday and Monday as our HC days, is that Sunday night is the slowest night of the week for any business hotel. The fact that we could fill Sunday night rooms was crucial, and made the Atlanta Sheraton want to work with us. Among the things we needed were late checkout times for our clients who were interviewing for the entire day, a reasonable rate for our candidate conference room, hotel rooms for us to use as a command center, flexibility on how many rooms we would fill, a late release date for the hotel rooms we didn't fill, and a significantly reduced room rate for the military candidates.

All in all, there were 17 different items that went into running an HC that the hotel affected and were included in our contracts. We used the same hotel in Atlanta from the day we opened until the day I retired. There was a handshake relationship between us, and we were flexible on things they needed from us as we were with them. I remember a situation where they came to us and had an opportunity to land a big piece of business, but it required us to sacrifice use of the large ballroom we typically used, which we were able to do. We also served as a reference for them when they were competing for business against other hotels. Having our hotel view us as not only being a good piece of business, but our relationship one that provided additional value to them mattered.

This relationship became even more important as we expanded, and used them as a reference. Other hotels wanted to work with us because we not only filled hotel rooms on a slow night, but also because the Atlanta Sheraton gave us such a great recommendation. We would eventually hold our HCs in cities across the country, on virtually any weekend we wanted.

We sometimes had interesting things happen at our HC - some funny and some not. Typically, large hotel conference rooms are adjacent or near each other, and the Sheraton was no exception. On occasion, our neighbors would have a function with food set up outside of their conference room. Well, sometimes our candidates would meander over with nothing better to do between interviews than sample their products, and sometimes do a lot more than sample. On occasion, there was a locust effect, which caused us to make sure in the future we told our candidates that our neighbor's food was not for them.

Recruiterware

The road that began with us trying to get software to help schedule our HC interviews, led us to develop our own software which we called Recruiterware (RW). We eventually hired our own programmer, Don Nowak, who was a magic man. He had the unique ability to differentiate what I really wanted from what I said I wanted. Even better, he could tell me what could improve upon my idea. He did this for everybody else as well. The list of things he worked on to create new capabilities was almost endless. RW became almost like a living organism, with ongoing enhancements created to help us capture and manage the nuggets of information on both candidates and clients to make better matches. It became so powerful that we sometimes thought we could sell it. But it was so specific to a military recruiting firm that only our competition would be interested, which obviously wasn't going to happen.

I do smile when I think back to the transition from our previous database and manual HC scheduling method. RW was initially called GlacierWare by our people, as rolling it out took time and there were certainly bugs that had to be worked through. However, when our people eventually saw what it could do to help them, they changed their tune.

Off-Conference Interviews

These were interviews that took place independent of an HC. They could either be a telephone interview followed by an onsite interview, or the interview could be set up at the facility, simply based on our recommendation. These tended to be more targeted interviews, where the interest level by both the candidate and client was stronger upfront than the initial interviews at the HC. Telephone interviews, while easy to set up, often had a way of being interrupted by ongoing events at the location of the interviewer. We ALWAYS had the candidate call the client, instead of the other way around, to make sure the interview happened without a snag. Relying on the client to initiate the interview was often a hit-or-miss proposition.

PowerHire

These were volume hire situations (think OC interviews on steroids) with important clients that had the focus of everybody in BMI. They occurred at a company's location, typically with senior people from the company participating. The clients paid for all travel, meals, and hotel costs, as they would for any second interview. Often there was a reception held for the company representatives to be able to get to know the candidates in a more relaxed setting. These initiatives often ran from 20 placements to more than 100. Initially, and for a number of years, these had been called Mini-conferences. I hated that term because there was nothing mini about them. One day I got with Bill Scott, our Director of Marketing, and told him we just had to come up with a better name for them. We ended up incorporating "power' into the new name, PowerHire, which was both catchier and more accurate. Mini-conferences, hence, became known as PowerHires. I loved it.

Offers and Placements

Understandably, our candidates wanted to wait to make a decision until they had multiple offers in hand. The pressure from clients to fill their openings frequently made this part of the process messy. Candidates could often balance two, or sometimes even three, competing offers. However,, they frequently had gone on other interviews, with uncertainty as to whether an would be forthcoming. Candidates were then faced with accepting or declining offer(s) in hand, before they knew whether they would even get an offer from the other companies that had showed some interest. We did our best with this, and always made sure we never managed the data by withholding any information from either the candidate or the client. Transparency was the key. We explained to the candidates that the companies had real openings and needed them filled and, if it wasn't going to be them, the client needed to move on to the next person.

Among the things we tried to explain to the candidates were the different areas to consider in making the decision. These were location, money, type of job and company, upward mobility, and who your co-workers would be. We really tried to get the candidates to trust their instincts. Too many military candidates would think the civilian world was totally different, and not use their well-developed ability to assess and judge situations and people quickly and accurately. Typically, the candidates focused on money and location, as that was easy to understand. In reality, the people they would be working with was probably the most important variable and the least considered.

When candidates accepted offers and had activity with other companies pending, we required them to call those other companies to say they had accepted an offer were off the market. We wanted to eliminate the possibility of the candidates changing their mind about the company where they had just accepted the position, in the event the other opportunities came to fruition. This is not much different from a high school football player accepting a verbal offer from one college, just to have insurance, while continuing his recruitment. The difference here was that a candidate had officially accepted a position. A commitment had been made. Real lives and futures were at stake for both the client and candidate. We took that responsibility seriously.

Counteroffers

One of the biggest advantages we had over the civilian "search" firms was we almost never had to deal with a counteroffer. Once our candidates had made the decision to leave the service, they were on a predetermined schedule as to when they would become a civilian. The military was too big and too bureaucratic to come back to candidates, who had decided to leave the service, and offer more money or a promotion to convince them to stay.

Candidate Turns Down Offer

What happens when a candidate turns down your offer and goes to work at a company found on their own or through a competitor? At this point, it's over and you congratulate the candidate and say, "Good luck." We would tell the candidate we hoped we were helpful throughout the process, provided good information, and were supportive. Hopefully, this decision was not a surprise. Handling this situation well could yield additional candidate referrals, the candidate returning one day as a Hiring Authority, or possibly even changing their mind. You had to place yourself in the shoes of the candidate who was making the call. The fact that the candidate was professional enough to even make the call and notify you personally, instead of via an email or a voice mail, meant your relationship was of value. Getting upset with the decision just destroyed any positives that could come down the road, and told the candidate you only cared about yourself.

Aftercare

When my mom passed away, I was very impressed with the things the funeral home reviewed with my dad that had nothing to do with the funeral and the service. These were the details on things he needed to take care of with my mom's name on them. These included items such as car registration, Social Security, Medicare, and bank accounts, to name a few. I thought we should have something like this, so we established what we called our Aftercare Program. Since our ARs were now chasing the next placement and had never been very good at looking backwards anyhow, we had one of our support people take this on. She sent out guidance to the placed candidates on things they should do upon entering the civilian world (come in early and stay late to get off to a good start, be sensitive to others not having a military background, etc.), and made a call to them before they started in their new positions, as well as afterwards. We also made it clear that the candidates still represented us, we had expectations of them, and were pulling for them to be stars. This didn't yield any additional revenue, but it was a good thing to do. It felt right. It certainly let the candidates feel like we had not forgotten about them once they accepted a position, and that we still cared about them.

Job Orders

It was crucial our ARs got the right types of job orders from our clients and were committing us to those we could fill and not committing us to those we couldn't. Often an AR, especially our new ones, would hear what they wanted or needed to hear, and we would then have job orders we had little, if any, chance of filling. Keeping control of this was not easy. To minimize this problem, we looked at the types of job orders we were getting and created a color-code system for them based on ease of placement. Black was our sweet spot. We should be able to fill these positions 100 percent of the time. Blue was similar to Black with a single problem. It could be in a tough location or have a slightly lower salary than was standard for the position, but we should still be able to do it. Red had multiple problem areas. These could be in a bad location, very difficult to find candidates with the desired qualifications, a salary that was way too low or had other issues. I emphasized focusing on Black and Blue. We listed all of the job orders in their particular color on our RW homepage, which helped.

Over time, there was tension internally about business being left on the table with us not filling Red job orders, and I constantly had to fight this battle. I believed in focus, and trying to fill the exceptions took time away from the meat and potatoes of our business, which were the Black and Blue job orders. Creating a color-code system also educated our ARs as they could see they were not having much success with the Red job orders. Another crucial area was to correctly identify the location, and list if it was in a metro area or how far it was from one. For example, when a location is in Loganville, Georgia, saying it is in Metro Atlanta to a CR who doesn't know Loganville from Timbuktu, makes a huge difference.

We stayed away from filling sales positions for many years, because of my experience with sales job orders at TLG. I finally approved moving forward with placing sales candidates only when we were able to create Sales as a separate and unique Discipline. At TLG, I had seen over and over how the candidates who were more polished, had a better image and stronger communication skills, and were most often headed to sales positions anyway, take potential opportunities from candidates who would have taken the manufacturing position had the opportunity been available for them. It was hard for us to not allow "sales" candidates to interview for manufacturing positions, even though we might have thought they wouldn't take the opportunity, as they typically said all of the right things about being interested.

The following scenario too often occurred. Let's say a company interviewed 10 candidates and liked six. The top three might be more "sales" types, who might not take the position, and the candidates who were ranked numbers four through six would. The company almost never would follow on five and six, and four might get a shot. However, if the "sales" people had not been in the lineup to begin with, four through six would have been ranked in the top three, and would get second interviews. I also saw how making sales placements was simply harder. The interview process was inefficient. While the same number of interviews as on any other site visit would occur, they were often held on different days and in different locations as the sales managers, trainers and recruiters, who would conduct the follow-up interviews, tended to be travelling or were working in different locations. Conversely, not having sales positions available made our HCs more focused and efficient. We didn't have to deal with the "sales" candidate, because we didn't have any sales opportunities for those candidates.

When we did eventually establish Sales as a separate Discipline, it was successful because we went into it with our eyes open, knowing the landmines. By having a separate HC for them, and even its own location (Charlotte), we attracted only those candidates who were truly interested in sales, and eliminated the entire window-shopping experience for those who weren't sure about it, which was most of them. The clients loved it. Military candidates who go into sales tend to be superstars, or they fail miserably. The stars typically had no prior sales experience, but would do what it took to be successful because that was all they knew how to do. Unlike their sales rep peers, they already had substantial leadership experience, so once they proved themselves as a sales rep, they made fantastic sales managers, which is one of the reasons they were of such interest to Corporate America.

On balance, staying away from Sales and keeping focused on the technical leadership world for many years, was one of the smartest decisions we ever made.

Conference Coordinator Qualification Boards

CC was the most demanding position in our world. While having more than 70 companies and 130+ candidates at an HC virtually ensured we would make a lot of money, each company and candidate had no tolerance for their own customized schedule being wrong. With 600+ interviews taking place in one day, along with all of the unscheduled things that occurred, it took a level head and a lot of smarts to pull it off.

The military has qualification boards that serve as a final check before a person receives a major qualification. By the time of the board, the assumption is the person is qualified and passing the board is the final, yet most stressful, step before the official qualification is approved. The board is always comprised of already qualified people, who each ask a series of questions and pose multiple potential situations for the candidate to answer.

When I was on active duty, I was one of the first in Navy history to be awarded Navy Aviation Supply Officer Wings. This was a new program, and I was fortunate to be serving in a position that was a prerequisite for eligibility. The goal of the program was to improve the professional expertise of officers supporting naval aviation. However, naval aviators are very proud and protective of the "wings of gold" they wear on their uniform. Hence, anybody earning their "wings" was going to have to deserve it. After a year in my position, I was ready. My board consisted of four Navy Captains and the senior air wing maintenance officer. They made me answer a lot of tough questions, and when I passed I also knew I had a lot more to learn. However, I knew I had accomplished something that was very difficult and was proud to have been among the first to have earned the right to wear them.

We used this model for our CC Boards. I wanted our CCs to improve their expertise and feel the same sense of accomplishment I had felt. I sat on each board, along with a senior AR, senior CC, and the Discipline Vice President. Each was given time to ask questions. I always went last. One of the things I developed over the years was a comprehensive knowledge of military units, bases and organizations. I knew who they were, where they were, and what they did. You learn a lot by interviewing candidates on a daily basis from across the services. I always asked questions about the CRs territory he probably should have known, but I didn't think he would. I wanted to impress upon him the need to continue to study, and that he still didn't know enough. The last question I would always ask was, "Which of these three: the clients, candidates, or BMI people, was the most important?" The response was almost always the clients, because obviously they paid the bills. They never said the BMI people. I explained to them that this was wrong. Clients and candidates, while important and had to be taken care of, were not as important as the BMI people. Clients and candidates would come and go, but BMI people were your family. I wanted there to be no indecision on their part, if they had to handle the very rare situation of a client or candidate being inappropriate or overly aggressive with any of our people. The CCs were the on-scene commanders, and they needed to know we would never sacrifice our own people to chase placements.

I also wanted to find out why some of our people were better at managing all of the changes that occurred at an HC, and were mentally nimble enough to ensure the HC interview puzzle did not collapse. I looked at college transcripts and, while there were exceptions, I found that people who had strong math grades or had been in units with fast-moving military equipment (airplanes, tanks) seemed to do better.

Sending and Receiving

When I started with TLG, there were two military recruiting operations. One was in Atlanta, and the other was in Dallas. They tended to operate independently from each other and, in many ways, were in competition. Breaking down those barriers and changing each operation into viewing the other as a teammate instead of a threat was the single biggest thing we did to cause the number of placements to explode. We created a system for sending and receiving clients and candidates at HCs across regions.

Since 100 percent commission salespeople guard their clients with a death grip, we figured out a way for them to be motivated to send their client companies to HCs in the region that they would not normally attend. The driver of all of this was ensuring the original ARs, who had broken or were managing the mother relationship, would not lose any money when sending a company to another region. They were able to use their initial success to penetrate the rest of their client company in a way that a new person in another region would never have been able to do, as they already had a relationship with the client company. This then increased the total number of companies attending ALL of our HCs. It was also important the AR who sent their client to another HC have confidence their client would be taken care of, the brief would be done well, and the candidates would be qualified. To fund this system, the CRs at that HC would take a slight financial hit, but there were almost always double or triple the number of ARs than there were CRs, so it was more than fair. Besides the more companies that were at their HC, the more placements the CRs would make anyway, so they were all for this system.

Clients which had previously been engaged in only one region of the country were soon sent to other regions. This system also worked for candidates who might have been stationed on one side of the country, but wanted to live on the opposite coast. We also paid the ARs and CRs for their duties in receiving both clients and candidates and taking care of them. This system required a lot of teamwork and trust, but it was like pouring gasoline on a fire. It was magical. As with most really good ideas, this was almost too simple and too obvious, but it was the execution that was the key. Once this structure and culture was in place, this system simply continued, as if it had always existed, when additional offices were created. There was no need to "sell" the advantages of this system to our BMI people. This was part of our plan from the day we opened, and our people never knew any other way.

CHAPTER 4

Numbers and Analysis

We had a lot of moving parts. As time went on, I felt the need to try to get a better handle on what was happening and, more importantly, why it was happening. Delving into the operational numbers in detail provided me with many of the answers. I found the best way to find our numbers was to personally create and generate the reports, including entering the raw placement data myself.

We had much of the information on who we placed and where we placed them from the invoices we had sent to our clients. At about year five, I went back into the actual candidate files and HC grid sheets and created a separate placement database. I entered the information from EVERY placement we had ever made into over 30 different data fields that included candidate name, college, major, service, base, military specialty, company placed, position, salary, location, fee, gender, diversity, and on and on. While it may seem like something we should have already done, and with today's technology it would be very easy to do, back then it was not. While capturing this data was important, what was of equal importance was that I entered this data myself. It was a lot of work, and continued to be, as I entered this data into my own database every day until the day I retired.

The benefits to me were enormous. I was able to know every day, and pretty much every hour, what our sales were. I knew who was making placements and who was not. I knew the patterns and rhythms of our business. This effort enabled me to answer the basic questions of why things were happening, and even more importantly, create new questions to be asked. Had I been fed this data, I know I would not have learned it as well. It was entering this data myself that made the difference.

One of the things that is endemic to sales is that salespeople hear what they want to hear. In our business, this typically happened when an AR was getting a job order from a new company, but the company wouldn't or couldn't attend the HC. The company would invariably want to see some candidate resumes, and a lot of work was often done with very little result. However, it is very difficult to tell a recruiter, especially a new recruiter, that a particular job order is not worth their time, because there are exceptions. Since we made about 25 percent of our placements OC, filling these job orders was a big part of our business. However, I went back and analyzed every OC placement we had ever made and compared it to the HC interview matrix. I was able to show my people that 95 percent of the OC placements occurred ONLY with a company that had attended an HC first.

Essentially, this meant that despite what the company said, the reality was they weren't going to use us unless they had first attended an HC. If they wouldn't attend, they were wasting our time. As a result, I didn't allow my people to accept a job order unless the company first attended an HC, and I had the numbers to back it up. This then forced my people to sell harder to convince their client to attend the HC or freed up their time by not accepting job orders from potential clients who would not attend.

I also stumbled across an almost algorithmic number, which changed the game. While experimenting with how some numbers affected others, I divided the annual sales by the number of companies that had attended HCs in a particular year. I then checked the other years and, to my amazement, this number was accurate plus or minus 10 percent for every single year and continued to be for every year until the day I retired. I then was able to project our annual sales (all placement income regardless of method) based on how many companies would attend our HCs in the upcoming year.

The importance of companies attending the HC was already known, but this number made it THE number and the key to our business. Companies that attended the HC led to OC placements, volume hiring, and the ability to send companies to HCs across the country. This seems obvious, in retrospect, as the clients had spent time with us and had experienced success, which led to relationships and more business and more subsequent success. However, the emphasis and singular focus on this number was not present before. This led to us doing more HCs and hiring more ARs. I became fixated on that number. The bigger that number, the more placements we made. Pretty simple and, of course, we needed the candidates to support that effort, but one number drove everything.

I found that 20 percent of the companies provided 50 percent of our placements. Again, this was not surprising as internally we had called these machine accounts. But it did highlight the need to "make hay while the sun was shining," and make as many placements as we could with those companies while they were on a hiring binge.

One thing I noticed in doing the numbers was that once a company's annual placements with us peaked and started to decrease, there was no reversing this slide. The number of annual placements always, and I mean always, eventually went down to zero. While this seldom happened overnight, it always happened. Why? This was probably for a number of reasons: their need for hiring had been satisfied, there was a new hiring authority, the company's sales were down, layoffs were happening, we had done something wrong, or we had done something to upset them. The point was it always happened, which underscored the need for my people to have a variety of clients, not be dependent on only a few, and constantly seek new companies. Many of these companies would eventually return to working with us, but their hiatus, for whatever reason, was a fact of life our ARs had to anticipate and adjust accordingly.

I also looked at who WE were hiring and who had been successful. At year eight, I went back and reviewed the backgrounds of every single person we had hired, identifying who made it and who didn't. I looked for things that were common in either case. The results were startling and not what I had expected. We had assumed a prior sales or recruiting background or military experience were determining factors, but they were not. What we did find were three things that in every case determined future success, and the person had to have all three.

First, our successful people were likeable and had good communication skills. This may seem obvious but, in the past, we hired some people who had a strong resume, which clouded the fact that they just weren't very likeable. In our system, every person had to be able to function as part of a team, and candidates and clients needed to be able to connect with them. Second, it really didn't matter what their prior experience was. It only mattered that they had been the best at something. A person who has tasted excellence likes it, and likes it a lot, and will do what it takes to taste it again. Third was what we called the baggage factor. Why did people who had the first two qualities not make it? Without exception, there were issues that dragged them down – a long commute, an unsupportive spouse, debt, family problems, and on and on. Sometimes these things were not easy to learn, but if we listened and looked for it during the interviews, we could find it. As a result of these findings, I had all of my people rank every single prospective BMI employee on a scale of 1-10 in all three categories. While there was not a set criteria as to what determined the numerical score, it nonetheless focused my people on those areas and made them aware of where to look.

I looked at how our successful ARs had performed early in their careers. Without exception, they made placements and brought in clients to our HCs in substantial numbers. As a result, we established a minimum standard new ARs had to reach or we knew they weren't going to make it. We combined the number of placements they had to make along with how many companies they were able to get to attend an HC into one number. This mark was four by 90 days from their start date and nine by 120 days. These standards were then communicated and well understood.

Once we had expanded across the country, we brought all of our managers and senior people into Atlanta for annual meetings, during which we discussed the previous year and made plans for the upcoming one. I prepared what became known as "The Book," which included detailed operational statistics for the year, as well as an historical comparison on key numbers from the beginning of BMI.

As most statistical summaries are boring to read, especially for a group of salespeople, I didn't really expect them to examine it in detail. Instead, I used "The Book" as a vehicle to do a sales job on my own people. I tried to sell them on doing those things that would help THEM and, in the process, help BMI. It didn't seem to be enough for me to lecture them on what I wanted them to do. They had to see why I thought these were good ideas and how it would benefit each of them. The things I emphasized changed over time, but here are some examples:

• Ninety percent of our placements came from our targeted or profiled candidate group. There was always the tendency for a CR to work candidates outside of the groups we targeted, but we just didn't place very many. They needed to be reminded where to spend their time.

• We could only place geographically-restricted candidates into certain metro areas. By highlighting those areas, I could show my people how they were not only wasting their own time, but the candidates' time as well, if they wanted to live in an area we couldn't service. (Atlanta, Dallas and Chicago were fine. Seattle and Orlando were not going to happen.)

• I was able to show them the importance of PowerHires and how many placements had resulted from them. I wanted us to do more of them, but needed my people to see how successful they had been.

Shaun G. Bradley

CHAPTER 5

Sandy

My co-founder was Sandy Morris. I've often thought one of the mistakes people make is to go into business with their buddy. The problem, oftentimes, is that person is just like them with a similar outlook, background, and skill set. Sandy and I went back to our days together at TLG. While she did not work in the military group, she had been successful in another staffing area, and had left the company about a year earlier than me to form her own company. We had always gotten on, and while she was not ex-military, she certainly had a military appreciation, as her father had been the youngest member of his battalion to jump with the 82nd Airborne on D-Day. He also took part in Operation Market Garden, the Battle of the Bulge and, eventually, his unit met the Russians on the Elbe River. Very similar to the road the Band of Brothers travelled.

Sandy's background was extraordinary. Valedictorian and president of her high school class, she was awarded a full academic scholarship to college, graduating from Eastern Illinois University in just three years. She was also a killer salesperson.

Our skills and background really fit together: male/female, military/non-military, CR/AR, very organized (her)/not so much me. Even though she did not have any prior military recruiting experience, she was a quick learner. We put the same amount of money into the business, dollar for dollar, and were paid the exact same amount throughout our time together. There were never any issues about who was working harder or contributing more.

There was a seminal moment early on. Sandy had some business from her former staffing company that she finalized after we had opened, and I didn't feel like I should share in that money, as I hadn't done anything to earn it. She was insistent that we were together now, and that whatever was done would be shared. This set the tone for how we would share things and operate together in the years to come.

Sandy made the trains run on time in our company, and while she had primary responsibility for our internal business machinations (finance, legal, payroll, banking, insurance, leases, etc.), there were still many things in her area where I had involvement, as did she in operations and sales. This was especially true in the early days, when she brought in some of our most important clients, including General Electric (GE), Cargill and Wal-Mart.

While we had our share of disagreements over the years, we always kept each other's confidences, and I was always able to trust her. I also liked having somebody who was cooking in the same pot as me, and had the same consequences if things went bad. I also valued that Sandy took on primary responsibility for many things I either had little aptitude for or didn't like to do. As I look back on my partnership and relationship with Sandy, I know in my bones that BMI would never have become what it became without the both of us. Nobody at BMI valued Sandy more than I did. I can well remember when Sandy was on maternity leave, and I had to make sure payroll was done correctly. Sandy left me five pages of detailed step-by-step instructions on how to do it. The entire time she was gone I was thinking, "Thank God, I don't have to do this every payday." I knew, if I had made a mistake, I would have never heard the end of it with my people saying, "Thank God Sandy is back! Shaun really screwed up payroll."

As BMI grew, our roles evolved with both Sandy and me moving away from placement generation. She continued to focus on the crucial infrastructure areas. I spent my time on operations and sales, although Sandy continued her vital involvement in training and hiring. When you're in a partnership, you can only disagree so much, so you learn to pick your moments. Hence, I picked my spots when I disagreed with something in her area, as did she with mine. If I could do what I wanted to do, and the rest was 90 percent of the way I wanted it to be, I figured that was pretty good.

BMI became Bradley-Morris instead of Morris-Bradley when we opened because I was a recognized name in the military recruiting industry, while Sandy was not. Our titles were all over the map. We started as Managing Partners and Co-founders and then I became President and Sandy became Treasurer, as she was more involved with the money. Then, because we were a corporation, our attorney said we needed to have a CEO so that is what I became and Sandy continued as Treasurer. In 2005, we changed titles again and we became Co-CEO's. There was never, and I mean never, any decision that both of us did not have to agree on, so titles may have been significant externally, but they meant little to me.

Shaun G. Bradley

CHAPTER 6

The Lucas Group

I owe a lot to Art Lucas[3] and TLG, and always will. I met my wife there, got my start there, had great times there, and still have friends I made there. They are a great company, which does things right. In business, you are fortunate if you have a major competitor you respect as much as I did them.

First Placement

The first placement I ever made was also the easiest placement I ever made and it happened my first week. I had met the candidate in the early morning, and sent him on an interview for a sales rep position with Gallo Winery later that same morning. He called me after lunch to let me know he had been hired. I doubt I ever had a more perfect candidate for any position, and I remember telling my boss, "What's so hard about this?" The candidate was an Army Airborne Captain, who had just returned to the states after having been in the elite 173rd Airborne located in Vicenza, Italy. He had played defensive back in college and looked like a million bucks. Gallo Winery (like virtually all consumer product companies) loved college athletes. He also had a fiancé whose parents owned a vineyard in Italy. He was a bullseye fit to say the least. There would be a long dry spell before I made my second placement and it would not be so easy. I was learning.

---

[3] Founder and long-time CEO of The Lucas Group.

Separate Sales Chart

During my time at TLG, it almost felt like we were minting money. We were making placements at a rate never done there before. TLG actually changed the sales chart because of the Military Group. Previously, the top ten billers in the company had been highlighted. Soon nine of these 10 were my military people. Eventually, two separate sales charts were created, one for the military group and one for everybody else. The rest of the company couldn't compete, and others in the company complained that recruiting military was easier. (A far cry from my first day, when I was told nobody ever made any money recruiting military.)

Not a Fit for Military

TLG's compensation plan was not structured for how the military group recruited. Unlike the rest of the company, the military group had a defined division of labor between those who recruited candidates and those who recruited companies. However, our system required more people to bring in the companies than it did to recruit the candidates. With each placement being split evenly between the candidate and client side, this resulted in the CRs making a lot more money than the ARs. Hence, a CR was always at the top of the sales charts. When we started BMI, to make this more equitable, we made the AR commission rate higher than that of a CR. We couldn't really adjust how many people we needed to perform each job, but we could make sure their pay was more in line.

Fun in a Corporate Environment

While at TLG, I learned how to have fun in a corporate environment from my boss, Carol Rifkin. Reward lunches, movies, days at Lake Lanier, charades, anniversary songs, and parties were all part of it. Maybe it was her, maybe it was because we were all young and single, but it was a fun place to be. Being committed and focused on getting the job done was the key, and having fun only made us work harder.

Multiple Locations and Multiple Branches

As BMI grew, I took advantage of going to a talk Art Lucas gave while he was President of the Georgia Association of Personnel Services (GAPS), the umbrella organization for the Georgia staffing industry. He was providing guidance on managing multi-state, multi-Discipline operations, which was the direction we were headed. When he saw me, he asked what I was doing there. I told him I wanted to learn from the master. He said, "You already learned too damn much the first time." Funny.

Shaun G. Bradley

CHAPTER 7

Growing Up

Green Bay was an idyllic place to grow up. Church, family and school formed its backbone. As I look back, there were defining moments that impacted me, which directly affected how I led and ran our business. I became very good at identifying opportunities and seizing them. I internalized lessons on important virtues, such as loyalty, saving money, not quitting, and bad decisions having consequences, and never forgot them.

The Depression

My parents were Depression-era children and never lost the feeling that a bad day could come and you had better save for it. My dad was a maintenance man who worked two jobs to pay off his 30-year mortgage on our modest house (1,300 square feet bought in 1963 for $15,000) in 12 years. My Mom worked as a proofreader for the local newspaper to provide extras. Having the security of jobs and no debt was everything to them because they had experienced what real hardship was.

My dad grew up outside of Green Bay on a farm that is still in the family and today is run by my cousin. During the Depression, they fed many people passing through who were struggling even more than they were. My dad often told me about eating lard sandwiches. My grandfather was a hero in their world, because he had a job with the Wisconsin Public Service. He had a job!

My dad was physically tough. As a young man, his heel had been crushed when he was run over by a manure spreader. Alone in the field, he crawled to the large family farmhouse, where the doctor was called.

His foot never really healed properly, and yet he worked on his feet for his entire life, never complaining and never missing a day of work! I vividly remember seeing his black-and-blue foot after he removed his sock from the foot that had been injured.

Loyalty

My grandfather told me a story that is seared in my memory and one I have retold many times. I was 16 and was with my grandfather one day when we went into a store (about half the size of a 7-11) to buy groceries. It was operated and owned by a guy who was even older than my grandfather. This was an old-time store, where you told the person behind the counter what you wanted and then were given it.

I made the mistake of making a smart-aleck comment to my grandfather about going into a place like this to get food. He then said, "Let me tell you a story. One year during the Depression, I fell off of a ladder and broke both heels and couldn't work for a year. That old guy, who runs this store you don't seem to think much of, gave me credit to buy food for a year, so your mom and aunt and uncle could eat. That's why I still go in there even today. Now do you understand why we're in here? You OK with that?" I was pretty humbled and, of course, said, "Yes Grandpa, I'm good with that." I never forgot how loyal my grandfather was, even 40 years later, to the man who had helped him out when he needed it most.

Consequences

My mother was a force. As she was a proofreader for the local newspaper, I would have been in less trouble for landing in jail than for using incorrect grammar or misspelling a word. She also meant business. I was caught smoking when I was 11. This was over the summer, and I was grounded for a month and only allowed to leave our house and property to go to my Little League games or practices. My friends could come over and see me, but that was it. The term "house arrest" would be accurate. I grew up not wondering what was right or wrong, and clearly understood there would be consequences for crossing the line.

Lambeau Field

As I mentioned earlier, I sold peanuts at Green Bay Packer games at Lambeau Field. I did this from seventh grade through my senior year in high school (1968-1973). It is hard to overstate how important this was to me in eventually starting and owning my own company. My box of peanuts had 100 bags in it and each bag sold for 35 cents of which I received four cents on each bag. I became the top seller (#1 of 72), selling 50 percent more than the next highest person. I would earn $24 for selling 600 bags.

I found out early that I looked at things a little differently from others. While all of the other guys were trying to hawk their peanuts to people as they were coming through the gate, and while that was where most of the people were, I didn't think their mindset was to buy anything until they were situated in their seats. I decided to go up and roam the stands. While there were a lot fewer people up there, they were ready to buy; I had them all to myself. I would sell two boxes before the game even started. Then I would sell one box while the game was going on, leaving in the middle of the second quarter to stake out a position outside of the men's bathroom, where I would sell a couple more boxes at halftime. When the third quarter started, I would go back in the stands and sell one more during the second half. I told my buddies how I did this, but as with many other things I would see throughout my life, they thought they knew a better way. It would not be the last time I would gain the advantage by looking at the world differently.

I also had a choice whether to sell peanuts or Cokes. Most of my friends picked selling Cokes, which was perceived as being a lot sexier than selling bags of peanuts, at least in the eyes of young teenage boys. The Cokes were sold on a tray, which had to be replenished more frequently than my box of 100 bags of peanuts. The trays were also messier and more unwieldy than my box of peanuts bags. In addition, selling Cokes when the weather turned was not as easy as it was during the summer and early fall. Selling peanuts was easier and I made more money. I didn't need sexy.

When I was 17, there was a moment when I was faced with doing what the West Pointers call "The Harder Right." I was given a box to sell that I knew had not been marked down for me. This meant I could sell the entire box and keep all of the money. The entire time I was selling that box, I knew I could get $35 instead of $4, if I kept my mouth shut. I really struggled with what to do, as an additional $31 in my pocket was a lot of money to a teenager in 1973, and would more than double what I would get in commissions for the entire game. On my way to sign out after the game, I still didn't know what I was going to do. They checked me out and gave me my money. I then told them they had not noted an additional box for me, and gave them the money for it. They said thanks and moved on. Maybe it was guilt or my Catholic upbringing that caused me to do it, but I gained tremendous confidence in myself. I knew I would not wonder what I would do the next time I faced an issue that required me to do the right thing. I knew.

There is no doubt in my mind that my Lambeau Field experience led me into commission sales. This was something I liked and wanted. I had tasted it. I loved the feeling that the harder and smarter you worked, the more you sold and the more you made. I also liked knowing there was a scoreboard, and your performance was judged on what you actually did and not necessarily how you did it. I learned performance gave you recognition and also the ability to do things your own way.

The Short Line

I played football for the first time when I was in ninth grade, at a very large school with more than 100 boys trying out for just the freshman team. Many of the kids went to the positions where you touched the football – quarterback, running back, and end. The big and slow ones (like me) went to the other large group. On the way to that group, I saw a really short line for centers with only two people in it. Even though I had never snapped a football in my life, I went there thinking it gave me the best chance, as I didn't really care where I played. I just wanted to get on the field and I went to where I saw the opportunity. I ended up playing center and nose guard that entire year and then the next year was switched to fullback and linebacker, where I stayed.

Rained Out

When I was 15, I had a baseball game scheduled for later that evening, and it had rained hard all day long. I mean a downpour. My coach had been insistent that he would let us know if a game was ever cancelled and to show up otherwise. In the afternoon, I started to get my baseball stuff together and put my uniform on. My mom asked me where I was going. I told her I was going to my game. She said there was no way I was playing. I argued with her and insisted my coach would have called if the game was cancelled. I rode my bike to the game and waited and waited. Of course, the field was virtually underwater. Only one person was on that field until after the game was scheduled to be played. Me. Was I the fool or was I the one who was going to show up no matter what? I still don't know, but I can tell you, I never missed a day of work in my life, unless I was in the hospital.

Shoveling Snow

For a number of years, I had a job shoveling snow for a rich family (at least rich in my eyes). I was always diligent and punctual and they could count on me. I was given $2 for doing their shoveling. One time, after they paid me, I walked home and had somehow lost the $2. I walked back to their house and knocked on the door. I told them I lost the money and asked if perhaps they found it on the porch. They said no and closed the door. I never forgot how that made me feel. I'm not sure what I even expected them to do – perhaps check around the porch or maybe even show a little empathy. I continued to do their shoveling, but never forgot how it felt to be taken for granted and not respected. I would never treat people who did things for me that way.

Coach Wall Knowing My Name

When I was in the eighth grade, my Catholic grade school basketball team was tops in the city. While it may not seem like much, given Green

Bay's winter, basketball is just about the only entertainment. As Green Bay is extremely Catholic with a lot of parochial grade schools, this was a big deal. I was one of the top players in the city that year. (Tom Anderson, who would go on to be a small-college All-American, was easily the best.) My parents wanted me to go to the Catholic high school across town, but were not insistent. However, playing football and basketball for the local public high school had always been my dream. The coach of the local public high school (Coach Keith Wall) approached me after a game and told me how well I had played. I left there thinking, "He knew my name, he knew my name!" I can't begin to overstate the importance to me of such a simple act. I ended up attending the public high school, and Coach Wall and I remain close to this day. I think in some way that affected how I recruited. I always made an effort to know something about a candidate that might make an impression on them. Doing something extra for a person or knowing something extra about someone has powerful effects. I learned that early in life.

Being Recruited for Football

After a good junior year in basketball, and especially in football, and getting letters from several Big Ten schools, I thought I would be going big-time in football. I thought I was better than I really was. But after I suffered a broken and dislocated ankle halfway through my senior season of football, everybody big who had been interested in me dried up, except for the Naval Academy. I'm sure I could have gone to college somewhere, probably to a small school in Wisconsin or Minnesota, and played football or basketball, since I was more athletically suited for that level. But attending USNA was the chance of a lifetime and too good of an opportunity to pass up. This was especially true for me, as there was little money in my family to go to college.

Almost Quitting

Perhaps my toughest experience in sports, and certainly in high school, was during my senior year of basketball. After starting every game of my junior year and averaging over 20 points per game in a summer league, I had rehabilitated the ankle I had injured in football and was ready to play by mid-February. Although I was physically ready, the team was clicking and Coach Wall (who is in the Wisconsin High School Basketball Coaches Hall of Fame) made a tough decision. He continued with the unit that already had success throughout the season, and would eventually come one game short of making the state tournament. I almost quit the team over not starting. However, I knew there would come a time in my life where somebody close to me, perhaps my children, would face a difficult situation. If I had quit then, I would not be able to tell them how I didn't quit when I was faced with some adversity. I was also aware this was a very difficult decision for Coach Wall to make, especially in light of our personal relationship. On some level, I respected that he made the tough decision based on what he felt was best for the team, although I didn't like it. I also did not forget when I was injured, none of my football coaches ever came to the hospital to check on me. Coach Wall was the only one who did. Years later, I was honored to be a guest speaker at his testimonial dinner.

Laying Sod

When I was a high school junior, I was on Prom Court and needed money to rent a tuxedo and buy my date a corsage. So my dad got me a job laying sod for a company a friend of his owned. I will never forget the older men I worked with, none of whom had any education. If I had any doubts about going to college before that experience, I sure didn't afterwards. Manual labor has a way clarifying one's mind. College led one direction and not getting an education led another.

Baling Hay

We lived on the family farm until I was in second grade. When my dad's father died, my dad had first dibs on taking over the farm. But my mom had enough of farm life and we moved to Green Bay. At age 40, my dad restarted his life as a maintenance supervisor for one of the major companies in the paper industry. However, farming and the work connected to it were part of the world in which I grew up. While in high school, one of my friends needed help baling hay on his family farm. We worked for a couple of days and it was a good workout over the summer, prior to starting football. We earned a penny a bale for loading and hauling 2,000 bales of hay, and I received $20 for the effort. Not much money for the amount of work we had done, but after we were finished my friend's mom fed us like we were kings. Even after all of these years, I can't believe how much we ate. I put away six half-pound hamburgers and easily drank a half-gallon of lemonade. At age 17 you can consume a lot. We were sitting at the table literally in agony we were so stuffed! My friend's mom then came out and asked, "Are you boys ready for some apple pie a la mode?" We told her, "Ma'am, no thanks - we're stuffed and can't eat any more." Stunned she said, "What's the matter? I thought you boys were hungry."

CHAPTER 8

Culture

Perhaps the most amazing thing about BMI was to have 100 percent commission salespeople not only work within a team framework, but to thrive in it. This is something most people in the staffing industry are stunned by when they learn what we were able to do. There were a number of things that made this possible. One was division of labor. Unlike most staffing firms, where the same person can work both the candidate and the client side and make what is called a double, our CRs and ARs were not permitted to work the other side of the BMI operation. Each needed the other. HCs also required a significant number of people providing candidates and clients to make them happen. No one could do it alone or even with only a couple of people. Another major factor was the significant amount of teamwork most of our people had experienced prior to arriving at BMI. They liked being part of a team. They didn't want to succeed alone.

There was an additional dynamic that enabled us to conduct the HCs. As the ARs were dependent on the CRs to bring in the right candidates, and the CRs were every bit as dependent on the ARs to get their clients to attend, each group felt tremendous pressure to not fail their counterparts. The pressure to deliver for their mates was powerful.

Contradictions

Our company was in many respects a series of contradictions. BMI was operationally very tight, but loose in structure. Commission salespeople worked together as a team. Seventy percent were ex-military, but we had a relaxed chain of command. There were operational and ethical principles, but few written rules. Most were men, but many of the top salespeople, including the co-founder, were women. Most were college graduates, but some of our best people had not completed their college degrees.

There were common threads that ran through our people. They had tasted excellence somewhere along the way. Most were somewhat irreverent in both style and personality. The vast majority had a sports background of some type. While not many were at this level, we had a one person who had been on the National Championship Football Team at Florida State, and another who had won a gold medal on the 4 X 100 relay team at the 1976 Olympics in Montreal. We even had a college intern who would go on to be an NBA first round draft choice. (He took no mercy on me, and would block my shot during lunchtime basketball.)

Senior People

One of the most essential ingredients in making this system work, perhaps the most important thing, was that our senior and most successful people bought into the system. While we had rules regarding account protection and candidate territories, the reality was there would never be enough rules in place to police everything. Consequently, our senior people had be unselfish and show by example, how to resolve a conflict. Over time, an unwritten set of rules on how ARs were supposed to conduct themselves developed.

This entire system worked because, while our people liked the 100 percent commission opportunity to make a lot of money, they also liked not doing it alone. They liked having the friendships and camaraderie of being on a team. It took special people and they were. You breed your own when it comes to culture, and new people tend to take on the ways of doing business they see practiced around them. A good culture is self-perpetuating, but so is a bad one. This is why I never took it for granted that we could pull this off and make it go. I knew how fragile it really was.

Sometimes you get lucky with people. David Youngerman was a friend of mine from TLG days and his girlfriend, Sue Zieler, was looking for a new job. (They would eventually marry.) David didn't want her to interview with TLG and have to deal with any potential issues that might create, so he called me to see if we might be interested in speaking with her. Sue was as sharp as they come and was unbelievably talented. She became a superstar for us. It is hard to overstate her importance to the creation of our culture and the follow-on success of BMI. While Sandy was successful in breaking new accounts, many of our other early ARs struggled. Sue being able to convince major clients to attend our HCs showed the others it wasn't only Sandy who could do it. As, or more important, she set the tone for being unselfish. Whether it was sharing leads or providing ad hoc training, she guided our new people and showed them how to be both successful and generous.

We also got lucky with another one of our early stars. Bill Basnett, USMA '86, was the son-in-law of one of my neighbors. I first met him while at TLG, when we placed him at Keebler Cookies in Atlanta in a plant engineering position. He was looking to make a move and became one of our earliest employees. He was a natural, and over time took on many of my responsibilities, including running HCs. His abilities enabled me to transition my role from generating placements to solely that of company leadership. He would leave BMI in 1999 to start his own military recruiting firm, but his contributions during the early days and growth years were major and irreplaceable.

We were not the company for everyone and when I heard new BMI people complain about being on commission, I understood it, but didn't really respect it. Some people nod their head and say they understand what it takes to be successful in commission sales, but often they really don't. Commission sales is one step away from owning your own company with the risks that it entails, but also with the rewards. I didn't lose much sleep when new people didn't make it. I felt our training was good enough and the opportunity was open enough for them to be successful, if they were willing to pay the price.

Meetings

We were lean on meetings. Wednesday was meeting day. Sandy and I would always go to lunch together, and then at 1 p.m., we would meet with the senior managers. At 2 p.m., we would have a meeting with ALL of the managers (typically around 15), which would last for about 30 minutes. These times were set in stone and never changed. Of course, we would meet when needed to discuss various issues, but these were almost always informal and typically didn't last very long. I think we avoided the meetings dilemma that plagues many companies by simply seeing each other and talking together on a daily basis.

Learning from Each Other

During the recession of 2001-2004, our people compiled a list of things they were doing that helped them create business and get them through the tough times. Some of the ideas were unique, but most were just common sense. These were communicated company-wide so everybody could use the nuggets of wisdom.

We also tried to determine why placements weren't being made. We compiled a list of reasons why things had gone south. Some of these reasons were obvious, but underscoring them armed our ARs with information, which helped to improve our ability to make placements. The reasons fell into fairly broad categories, such as being too slow to schedule a follow-up interview, too slow with an offer, or too slow with follow-up information on how the interview went. Sometimes there had simply been a bad company interviewer. These were basic, but it was very helpful for our people to see the commonality in why things didn't work. This then enabled our people to get ahead of these situations when they saw them coming. The best thing, however, was to be able to advise our clients in advance, on the reasons why some clients were more successful than others in getting the candidates they wanted.

Support People in Attendance

One of the things we implemented was to have our support people attend an HC, so they could see the end result of what our people were doing each week, and then be able to better support them. It also gave them a sense of being a part of things.

Fun

We had fun. There was constant laughter. The best sense of a locker room mentality prevailed. The list of things we did together to have fun was almost endless, but included birthday parties, skits, gag gifts, company trips, college football games, bowling, movies, more parties, specially written anniversary songs, and more. We even had our own company basketball team and played three to four times each week at lunchtime.

Visiting Another Office

I was talking with a friend after returning from a visit to our office in Norfolk, and he asked me what I had done on my trip. I told him one of my people picked me up at the airport and we had breakfast together. I then went to the office, talked to the group and then we played basketball. Next, I had lunch with another group of people before returning to the office to do some training. After work, I went to a party the team was throwing, before spending the night at the home of one of my people. The next day, I went to the office and hung out, did some of my own business, went to lunch with some more people and a manager drove me to the airport to fly back to Atlanta. He looked at me with disbelief in his eyes and said, "That was your trip?" It struck me then how different and unique we truly were. I wanted to touch my people and have them touch me. I used to joke that anybody who worked for us for any length of time was ruined forever for working for a "real" company.

Stupid Human Tricks

We had a tradition when new people started. On their first day, they would do a Stupid Human Trick as a type of initiation. Over time, people were warned about this so they were ready. Some of the things they did were really out there, but were never offensive or made anybody uncomfortable. People would tell jokes, perform magic tricks, sing songs, or demonstrate some trick they could do with their body they thought was unique to them. It didn't really matter what they did. It only mattered that they gave it a go. It was a way for them to become part of the group. My oldest daughter knew about these and would often ask me, "Daddy, did anybody do a Stupid Human Trick today?" I think when she was younger, she thought I worked in a circus.

CR Camping Trip

About 30 of the CRs flew in from around the country, and we all went on a camping trip one weekend in the North Georgia Mountains. Stories about this weekend were told for years afterwards. We even managed to get a bit of training in over a campfire. After the training, one of my guys, a Naval Academy classmate of mine, and a good guy who had held a senior position as the Senior Supply Officer on a Helicopter Aircraft Carrier, told me he thought my job and his job while in the Navy were very similar. I told him while there were some strong similarities, there were a few fundamental differences. First, I said the government decided what his people were going to be paid. In our company, we decided. Second, I told him if he made a mess, whoever replaced him (jobs in the military are rotated every 18-24 months) would have to clean it up. Since I was in my position for years, I was pretty careful about making a mess in the first place, because I was going to be the person who had to clean it up. Last, and, most importantly, I reminded him that in the military, all of his people were subject to the Uniformed Code of Military Justice and had to show up for work or they would go to jail. In the civilian world, nobody has to show up. As a result, you better make sure your people feel they have a good deal and are going come to work. If my people didn't show up, it was game over for us. I never forgot that.

Physical Layout

Our office environment was an open bay. I always liked that. People could learn from each other by just listening to their mates. It also fostered open and easy communication. I suppose you could squeeze more people into office cubicles, but I never liked that arrangement. I worked in the bay for the first six years of our company. Most of the leadership I did was by example, and after their initial training, most of the follow-on training was done during the daily course of events. As for motivating people, I thought they could either get to work or watch me work. Counseling never seemed to do any good or make much difference. When we moved to our much bigger offices, I moved from the open bay to an office. While necessary, as we were growing and had offices in other locations, I hated being removed from the action. I also thought no one would come and see me. I thought maybe no one would need me anymore. I could not have been more wrong. However, I never moved my office down to where our corporate offices were. I wanted to be in the action, and while I wasn't in the bays, I was pretty close. I wanted my people to see me and touch me, and I needed to see and touch them.

Going Casual

We had a very loose environment in terms of what we wore in the office, and this was standard in all of our offices. We would always wear suits and ties at the HCs or when we went on client visits, but around the office, where clients did not typically come, it was casual. I mean very casual. I typically wore Docker shorts, a golf shirt, and tennis shoes year round. When I was at TLG, we had a contest where, if the branch made 100 percent of goal for the week, we could go casual the next week. We subsequently went casual for the next 26 weeks, which actually caused some problems for the other branches that were wearing suits in the same offices. I learned what you wore was not connected to performance.

Pride in Our Culture

We took pride in being a company that operated loosely. All types were welcome, as long as they did their job and did it well. There was irreverence for things formal and staid. The reality is, we were able to work with the best companies in the world, but we didn't have to live with them.

Manuals

Our written policy book and HR manual were pretty thin. Saying we had a comprehensive HR manual would be charitable, although over time, it did grow. For many years, when I was interviewing candidates to work for us, if I was ever asked what our vacation policy was I'd think to myself, "I don't want somebody coming into a 100 percent commission job, even thinking about vacation time." Typically, I would tell them, "I don't care. If you do what you're supposed to do, take as much as you want. If you don't do what you're supposed to do, it won't matter."

Camaraderie

The camaraderie of the unit has always been an important part of my life. My career took me from the Naval Academy to the Navy to TLG to BMI and to coaching. Frankly, the sense of being part of a team was easily as important to me as the money or even the type of job I was doing. I have told many candidates over the years that probably the most important thing in a job is who your workmates are. You can be in a great job, doing work you enjoy, making good money and be in a great location, but if you are around people you don't fit with, you will be miserable. On the other hand, you can be lacking most of those and doing incredibly hard and difficult work, but if you are with great people it can be one of the best experiences of your life.

Receiving an Annual Gift

To our surprise, Sandy and I received an annual gift from our people at our company Christmas parties. One year I even received a Green Bay Packer stock certificate. While I accepted these gifts graciously, it always made me a little uncomfortable, to even be given them.

CHAPTER 9

Account Management

Having ARs calling on any company across the country, and then sending those clients to HCs held in locations throughout the country, led to maximum penetration of those companies. It also virtually ensured that we would make a lot of placements. However, this system was fraught with landmines and had the potential to self-destruct. Consequently, we developed internal controls to help maintain some semblance of order.

I had a unique background in this area, being one of the few people in our industry to ever perform duties in all three distinct positions. While I had started my career at TLG as a CR, by the end of my first year I had the candidate recruiting train chugging along pretty well. However, we did not have enough companies attending the HCs to support the number of candidates I had. I went to my boss and asked her if I could do the AR side of the business as well. Not really knowing what I was doing, I launched in and broke some major accounts, including Procter & Gamble, Air Products, Gaylord Container, and Abbott Labs, among others. Adding to this was that I also ran HCs, which would pay future dividends in giving me the perspective to balance the needs of our clients, our candidates, and my own people for the rest of my career. I also had the confidence to guide and lead our ARs that only comes from making the cold calls and managing clients.

Account Protection

We initially thought assigning our people to specific industries was the way to go, but soon enough realized we didn't have the research, background or knowledge to accurately pick industries for our people to pursue. Freeing our ARs to go after whatever companies they wanted to target proved to be a much better option. The downside of this decision was our expertise in specific industries was never as good as it might have been had we been more focused. But, as our candidates were for the most part going into entry level positions that didn't require in-depth industry expertise, the trade off was worth it.

When our AR numbers were small, we allowed them to identify the specific companies they wanted to go after, so as to not collide with their fellow ARs. This worked well until we grew and there were then a lot of companies that were listed as being worked, but really weren't. This became a rainy-day list, which prevented new people or other ARs from going after those companies.

We wrestled with modifications to that system without much luck, and finally did the obvious. We went to our senior people and explained the problem, of which they were well aware, and asked them to give us a solution. The guidance we gave them was pretty broad. Give us a system that protects ARs for the work they have done, while keeping things open for new people and other ARs to be able to go after companies that aren't actively being worked. In retrospect, it was too easy. They came back to us with an account management system they called the ABAL, short for Activity Based Account List. This new system only provided account protection for work that had been done - not for what might happen. Getting a company to attend an HC provided protection for a certain period of time, with increasing levels of protection for an increasing number of placements made over a defined period of time. No more rainy-day lists. This system, with slight modifications, remained in place through the day I retired.

Cross-Selling

While our system of sending clients to HCs across the country worked like a charm, our focus on creating new and separate Disciplines had its downside. Something new can be threatening when people are successful in one area and are reluctant to risk their already established relationships on something new and unproven. Consequently, some of our senior ARs sat back and waited to see if our new operations would work before they got onboard. (I periodically had lunch with Art Lucas and I explained this problem to him. I asked him how he dealt with this issue. He said, "Let me know when you figure it out!" So we weren't unique in having this issue.) We did identify this potential problem in advance and transferred some of our current ARs, as well as hired new ARs, specifically for each new Discipline, which helped. Our senior ARs eventually jumped onboard when we showed success in the new areas.

When we created a new Discipline, we mandated it have its own distinct HCs. The choice to have separate Officer and Enlisted Disciplines (and later on IT/Telecom), at separate HCs on separate dates, and even in different locations, forced each to grow strong in its own right. This would never have been the case if the new effort had been attached to a proven and already successful operation. For example, our Enlisted recruiting operation, which was new to us in the late '90's, ended up annually placing three times the number of Officer placements. The other advantage to not lumping Officer and Enlisted candidates together at the same HC, was avoiding chemistry issues with the Officers interviewing for management developmental positions and the Enlisted candidates interviewing for technician and field service positions. There was some carryover where senior enlisted candidates were qualified for the management positions, but not much. At each HC, both types of candidates were made to feel they were the priority and focus, because they were.

Golden Geese

I viewed my ARs, the business development people, as the golden geese laying the golden eggs. The ARs were the ones with the client relationships, who were bringing in the job orders and getting their clients to attend the HCs. As I had done that job while at TLG, I knew only too well how hard it was to get a client to attend an HC for the first time. Building on that relationship and having them come to future HCs, and then using that same relationship to penetrate the other areas and divisions of the company, took a lot of talent. I also knew how hard it was to find people who were willing to take the risk that working for us entailed and then be good enough to do it and do it for a long period of time. This is why again and again, I erred on the side of loyalty to them, and really did everything I could to help them and love on them. For most of them, making cold calls was hard. Some were better at this than others, but no one likes making cold calls and dealing with rejection. In our company, the CRs eventually rose to the leadership positions (although Sandy had always been an AR), but the ARs were the key and very, very difficult to replace.

Rewarding Positive Behavior

While we had a national account system in place, there could never be enough rules and protections to cover every situation. Inevitably, there were conflicts, where things ideally were resolved by the parties involved. Sometimes the dispute was elevated, and a manager would make the decision. But often each person had their own manager advocate for them. Typically somebody would take the high road and have one in the bank for the next time. ARs did not want to get a reputation as being selfish or not a team player, which, in our company, was a very bad thing. We tried to make sure the person who took the high road received some sort of positive recognition. This typically involved a conversation acknowledging we were aware of what happened and what they had done. In addition (and this was never talked about or addressed), I would remember these and would throw a bone their way when I could. Typically, there would be a call-in of some sort where a company wanted to use us. The standard procedure was for these to go on rotation, but sometimes I just skipped that entire process and gave it to the person who had taken the high road. I never explained why I was doing it, but I think at some level they knew.

Splits

Occasionally, I was approached by other recruiting firms, some military and some not, about the possibility of doing splits. If they provided us with a candidate or client, and if a placement occurred, we would each receive half of the fee. I always turned them down. While it might have resulted in the occasional placement, it would have opened Pandora's box with my people then not being solely dependent on each other for their success.

Major Hiring Initiatives

Jack Welch (then CEO of GE) wrote in his book, "Jack, Straight From the Gut," about GE's discovery of military officers as a great source of talent. "In 1995, Bob Nardelli, CEO of GE Transportation, described a new source of great talent. With its headquarters in Erie, Pennsylvania, the transportation business had struggled for years to attract the best people. Bob said he had found an endless supply of talent in junior military officers (JMOs). Most were graduates of U.S. military academies who had put in four to five years of military time. They were hardworking, smart and intense, had leadership experience and were surprisingly flexible because they had served in some of the toughest places in the world. Nardelli's idea spread like wildfire. After we had 80 former JMOs on staff, we asked them to come to Fairfield for a day. We were all so impressed with the quality of what we saw that we put a plan in place to hire 200 of them every year."

Four major military recruiting firms (BMI, TLG, CDC and Orion) were hired to support this effort. Remarkably, GE told us to write our own rules and figure out how to work together. They didn't want to police us. To some degree, we were scorpions in a bottle, being ultra-competitive with each other. For the most part, we got along. I remember commenting to the other firms that there was so much business here, it was akin to going into a large grocery store with each of us starting to eat in a different aisle. If we ate everything in our own row, it would take years before we even saw each other and to not be greedy. There was enough business for all of us. We made hundreds of placements with GE, and we were not alone. This effort lasted for years.

Fast-forward to 2002. We were knee-deep in the recession of 2001-2004. Sales had cratered. Bob Nardelli did not get the top job at GE, and moved on to be the CEO of The Home Depot (HD), where he initiated a similar program to the one at GE. Again, there was an initiative to hire JMO's, but this time not all four military recruiting firms would be used. Sandy and I, along with one of our top people, went down for the big presentation at HD headquarrters in Atlanta to get that business. Our lead AR had a goatee and, to my surprise, had not shaved it off prior to the meeting. I was concerned that HD might be looking for a clean-shaven outfit, as they were so focused on hiring military people. I expressed my concern and my AR asked me, "What do you want me to do - shave it now?" I said, "Yes, right now." He responded, "Where am I supposed to do that?" By now, we were in the car headed down to the meeting. I told him, "We are going to go to a gas station and you're going to get a razor and go into the bathroom and shave off that goatee." I know he thought I was out of my mind, but we pulled into a gas station and the problem was solved. We were going to get that business.

Our presentation went well. The HD rep was a woman who knew me, and apparently had interviewed to be part of BMI a few years earlier, although I didn't remember her. I learned afterwards she really liked us, although I didn't know it at the time. At the end of the presentation, I told her since she was going to pick multiple firms, it was important that whoever she picked got along with each other, because if they didn't, guess who would be policing them? She asked, "Who?" I said, "You." She asked who we wouldn't want to work with, and I said we would never speak poorly about a competitor, so I didn't want to answer that question. She then asked who we would want to work with. I said we had a great relationship with TLG, as well as Career Development (a company we would acquire in the future). As we left the meeting, serendipity stepped in. TLG crew was arriving and we ran into them in the hallway and I saw Brian Trueblood, who worked for me for a number of years at TLG and had a big personality. With the HD people there, I went up to him and told him it was really a shame he had come all of this way because the HD people had just chosen us. There was big laughter from everybody, and the HD people saw the chemistry between the firms. BMI and TLG were chosen. I still shudder to think of what might have happened to BMI without that business.

That same year, we also did our first true joint venture (TLG again) with Daimler-Chrysler, which was looking to hire military candidates to address a bench strength issue. The TLG representative was Eric Stagliano (he of the borrowed shirt fame). We went way back together, as he was part of the first load of bricks that created their military recruiting machine. We made the presentation together, and the joint effort turned out to be a great success for both firms. Daimler-Chrysler ended up having a hiring event attended by senior people (which always makes a difference), and gave us each 24 slots to fill with candidates we selected. We would combine to make 29 placements (BMI made 16).

However, we almost didn't make the presentation to even get the business. The joint presentation with the TLG people was scheduled at Daimler-Chrysler headquarters outside of Detroit. I was driving the entire group in my Lincoln Navigator, and we were on track to be early for the meeting. I forgot about the the large luggage container on the top of my car and as we were driving into the parking garage, I hit the cement structure and couldn't go forward. The meeting was in 20 minutes, and while that luggage rack was expensive, it was a pittance compared to what the Daimler-Chrysler business was worth. I told Eric to get out of the car and see how much room we needed to get past what we had hit. We were about six inches too high. I told Eric to get in the car and told the others in the car to brace themselves for impact. One of two things was going to happen. We were going to break through or the luggage rack would be ripped off of the top of my car. Either way we weren't going to miss that meeting. The others were wide-eyed and I'm sure thought I was crazy. I backed the car up about 50 feet, floored it, hit the barrier, and squashed the rack down enough to get through albeit, with damage and scars I proudly left on that rack for the entire time I owned that car. We made the meeting.

West Coast Clients

With offices in multiple time zones, it became apparent that East Coast ARs were not calling on West Coast clients, even if they had a relationship established with that same company on the East Coast or in the Midwest. I heard a lot of reasons why this wasn't happening, but the reality was it was hurting our ability to have bigger HCs in Austin and San Diego. This created some angst when I wanted to open up the West Coast for our people in San Diego and Austin to call on those same companies. However, by digging into the numbers I showed the ARs they weren't losing anything they had or would probably ever have. I was able to show them we were still keeping faith with them, while still moving forward.

CHAPTER 10

Leadership Nuggets

"Nobody cares how much you know, until they know how much you care." Theodore Roosevelt.

This chapter describes many of the things I tried to do, observed, or learned while leading BMI. Some are unique, while some are standard leadership fare. Some I knew before we opened BMI, but many I only learned after being in the leadership position of a growing company.

Long View

I believe in taking the long view with people, to have them feel part of the team and proud of what they've done. Many people in leadership roles are driven and have Type-A personalities. They need and want to be challenged. Often your people aren't like that. Most are a bit insecure. Being repeatedly told what they need to do better frequently undermines their self-confidence and makes them even less effective. I have seen focusing on what they do well, instead of what they don't, to be the elixir, which leads to the improvement you want from them. I was accused early in my career of viewing things and people through "rose-colored glasses." While it wasn't meant as a compliment, I think that comment was pretty accurate. I tended to see and expect people to be their "best selves," and it served me pretty well.

The Pressure to Do It Again

All high-performing salespeople feel tremendous pressure to succeed again and again. Every time a new tracking period starts, whether it is monthly, quarterly or annually, they question whether they can actually do it again. It is very easy to take their top performance for granted, and not give them the shot of confidence that you believe in them and know they can do it again. Telling them you realize it was no picnic for them to achieve that high level can make a difference. I was able to put myself in their shoes. I never forgot when I was a frontline recruiter and put up numbers nobody had ever done before. Everybody else just assumed I would do it again and again. I wasn't so sure. I truly wondered if I could do it again, thinking maybe I just got lucky the last time.

Once People Made $100K

I saw people react differently to this. Some tried to figure out how to still make $100K and work a little less, while others tried to figure out what they could do to now make $200K. I was good with either. I was glad to have those who wanted to make $100K and never tried to pressure them to do more. It was a lot more effective to hire new people to grow the company, than it was to burn out and lose those who had already proven themselves and were satisfied with where they were.

Licking Their Wounds

In a people-only business, recruiting and retaining great people was really the game. Once I determined a new person was going to make it, my job really became helping them to succeed, cheering them on when they did well and, more importantly, helping them move on when they made a mistake or something went wrong. I wanted them to keep their confidence, and be able to re-enter the arena again and again and again. Daily failure was a part of our business, and even superstars failed, and failed often. This was not much different from a baseball player who will go into the Hall of Fame, even if he only fails seven out of 10 times at the plate.

In our world, new prospects said no and said no often. Old clients told us what we were doing wrong, candidates didn't do what they said they would do, and candidates we had vetted became anything but what we thought they were. ARs were on the frontlines and felt the full brunt when things did not go well. Our CCs were running HCs where there were 70+ clients and over 130 candidates with 600+ interviews that occurred in a single day. Not making a mistake was hard, and to do it again and again was even harder. My job was to encourage them and ensure they knew I understood how difficult it was. They needed to know I had confidence in them. I never said anything that wasn't true or I didn't believe, but helping my people lick their wounds to be able to enter the fray again and again was key.

Focus On What They Can Do

I had one person who was probably the greatest account breaker I've ever seen, and she could really manage relationships with her clients. The list of her conquests included General Motors (GM), GE, Ford, Merck and Applied Materials, among many others. She also had all of the intangibles you would want. She was a great teammate and had unbelievable integrity, but her administrative skills were less than stellar. However, she could do one thing better than anybody else. She could break major Fortune 500 Companies and get them to use us. This was arguably the most important thing in the company and I protected her. She was, in her own way, a genius and I focused on what she did well. I could find a lot of people who could do the administrative work. I couldn't find many people with the magic she had.

Complaints

One day I was in a meeting with the senior CRs and there was complaining going on about how much harder they were working than the ARs. The CRs typically worked longer hours than the ARs did. It was just the nature of the beast. ARs could only contact their hiring authorities during the workday. The CRs could call their candidates at night and on the weekend. However, the ARs had the much harder job, especially at the beginning of their careers. They had to cold call, while the CRs would have leads fed to them from call-ins or web hits or reply cards. Since I had done both jobs, I let it be known that I considered getting a company to attend an HC for the first time to be the hardest job in recruiting. Over time managing those relationships made that job easier and veteran ARs didn't spend much time cold calling. I didn't really care that much what hours the ARs worked, as long as they didn't abuse it too badly and got their numbers. The CRs were in the leadership positions so, in my mind, the standards were different for them anyway.

One particular CR was going on and on and on with his complaints. Finally, I got tired of it and told him, "You're right. I don't blame you for being upset. You have every right to be. There is no question you work harder than they do, so I'm going to solve this problem for you. Tomorrow you will be an AR." With his eyes bugging out his head and with sheer terror in them, he immediately cried, "No, no, no. That's not what I meant. I just wanted to point out what they were doing." He eventually begged me long enough so that I let him stay in his current position. I never again heard another unending complaint about the ARs work ethic from him or any other CR.

On a personal level, I wasn't very good at listening to complaints of any type. Dumping a problem in my lap, without addressing it thmselves or recommending a solution, just made me think the person who was complaining was the actual problem more than what they were whining about.

Time Starts When People Show Up

While stories about the "old days" can have their place in building a sense of tradition, if they're told too often, it makes anyone who wasn't there feel excluded or, worse, alienated. Nothing good comes from that.

Close to My People

I was very close to my people. I always considered it a tremendous honor to be invited to a wedding or to receive a graduation announcement. I never failed to attend, if I could, and send a check, even if I couldn't attend. I also made it a priority to visit any of our people who were in the hospital. I never forgot Coach Wall making that effort for me. After we promoted one of our top people and moved him to Norfolk, his wife and young son even lived with my family for about four months, so they could finish the school year in Atlanta. As I said, we were close. I was on the receiving end and was touched when a contingent from Atlanta braved a Wisconsin winter to attend my mom's funeral.

Base Trips

These were important were where our CRs would meet and interview prospective candidates. These trips often took a couple of days, and for many years, I always went with the CRs on their first trip to a military base in their territory. I was able to do some training but, more importantly, spent extra time with them to really make that connection.

Legendary Figure

Captain Bob Fenick was the Senior Supply Corps Officer for all of the aircraft carriers in the Pacific and was a legendary figure. On one of his visits to our ship, he made a special point to stop in to see me and tell me I was doing a good job. For him, it was probably a little thing. But, for somebody at his level to take the time, made a big impression on me. I never forgot the impact of a small comment by a leader and tried to remember to do the same thing.

Not Letting People Down

The trick in leadership situations is for the people you are leading to never want to let you down. But they have to feel like YOU won't let them down either, and you actually have to feel that way. You can't fake it. Most people, me included, will fail themselves, before they'll fail somebody else. The feeling of letting somebody down is so overwhelmingly negative, almost toxic for me, that I simply would do everything in my power to not let it happen.

I still vividly remember, while at TLG in 1988, screwing up the schedule for a candidate named Johnnel Dance. He had come to an HC specifically for an interview with Pfizer Distribution. He was not the only candidate they were interviewing that day, so we also gave him other opportunities to interview, but that position was the bullseye for him. Unfortunately, I made a mistake on the afternoon schedule and he was unable to interview with Pfizer at the HC. It was nobody's fault but mine, and I apologized to Johnnell for letting it happen. We made attempts after the HC to get him a phone interview, but I never forgot how devastated I was for letting him down.

Handwritten Notes

I am a fanatic on handwritten notes. I wrote a follow-on note to every client I ever met. While my own handwriting is not very good, it did have the silver lining of there being no doubt by any recipient that I actually wrote it myself. Sometimes I had more than 20 to write and, frankly, they were a pain to do. That is why they matter. Everybody knows it takes something extra to write one. They ALWAYS are read. No matter how much mail I received, I always read handwritten notes before anything else. Bad news never comes in a handwritten note – never.

My people knew this was a big deal for me and many of them adopted this practice over time. I also wrote personal notes to my people on everything – sales charts, placements, brief sheets, or anything else that came across my desk. I learned people kept a file of these and read them over and over again. I still have my own file. Only after I retired, did I then learn how much of an impact those notes had on my people. Even to this day, I receive notes from my former BMI people, telling me about how a handwritten note helped a candidate get a position or aided them in landing a client.

With the prevalence of email and texting and other electronic communication methods, the handwritten note is the most undervalued part of the entire interviewing process. Many hiring authorities are of a generation where these notes are valued and expected. They typically think receiving a thank you via email is a shortcut, albeit better than not receiving a follow-up note at all. When a client receives a handwritten note from a candidate, it now arms their new advocate with a weapon to help sell that candidate to the other people in the company. It pours gasoline on the momentum from the initial interview, and increases the odds that the follow-up interviews will take place.

Fork in the Road

There will come a time with every employee when they really need you. They might have a personal problem, they might be in a financial jam, or they just might need to talk. You have to recognize this as an opportunity. Unfortunately, these things always seem to happen at moments when you don't have the time or the money to make them your priority, but you better. This is a fork in the road, after which that person will truly know whether you value them or not. Regardless of what action you take, your relationship with that person will never be the same. It will be better or worse, but not the same. You either answered the bell or you didn't.

People's Children

If you do something for somebody's child, they really feel like they owe you in some way, and if you ever ask them to do something, they will almost always either feel obligated or glad to do it. I remember when I was travelling on a Delta flight to San Diego, which was basically an airborne cattle car. One of the flight attendants was the mother of one of my baseball players. She came over to say hello, after I checked onto the flight. About five minutes before the plane was scheduled to take off, I heard my name called over the loudspeaker, "Shaun Bradley, we have your upgrade to First Class." Nice.

Often it is as simple as being aware of what their children are doing or, as I had five kids, giving them some advice. When it comes to their children, people don't forget. Ever. I was on the other end of this when Sister Pat, the principal at my children's Catholic grade school, asked me to chair the Capital Campaign to build a new middle school and gym. This woman was a saint, and after all she had done for my children, how could I say no to her? Managing this campaign was not something I wanted to do, or thought I had the time for. However, I felt like I owed her, so, of course, I agreed to do it.

Your People Knowing You

I think it is important for your people to know you on a personal basis. This really hit home to me when I was in the Navy. I had taken over an area that had some issues. When an aircraft carrier deploys, only then does the air wing come onboard. Since I reported shortly before our deployment, I had not been able to spend time at sea with the air wing before we deployed. Consequently, when the air wing officers, who would be assigned to my area reported, I was new to them and vice versa. There were a lot of things that had to be fixed and fixed quickly. I got resistance and certainly learned some lessons on how to communicate better. When we pulled into port in Yokosuka, Japan, one of the young officers and I went to the base gym to play basketball for a couple of hours together. Afterwards, he told me, "You're a lot better guy than I thought you were." Obviously, this was a left-handed compliment, based on what he thought of me before, but it changed our relationship, and for the better.

Feeling of Confidence

Rear Admiral Mitchell showed a great deal of confidence in me, and I never forgot how that felt. When I met him for the first time, he told me he had always been #1 at everything he had done in the Navy (promoted early for every rank, MBA from the Wharton Business School after USNA). He expected my area to be #1 and to let him know if I needed his help. I left his office with a sense that he believed in me, and I would do what it took to prove his confidence in me was not misplaced. In retrospect, I think he probably told that to everybody, but I took it to heart. He was more confident in me than I was in myself. I learned how to do that with other people, and tried to make them feel like that towards me. My experience has been, if you give people some "sugar," they will do what it takes to get more.

Noticing People

One day I came across one of my people sitting at her desk, with tears running down her face. I asked her what had happened. She told me she thought she had done something wrong and I was mad at her. I told her I didn't know what she was talking about. She said I had walked past her in the hallway and didn't say hello or acknowledge her, so she thought she had done something she shouldn't have. I told her I must have been thinking about something else and hadn't seen her. I told her I was sorry, and she hadn't done anything wrong. Now, obviously, she was hyper-sensitive and a bit overly dramatic. Nonetheless, that episode reminded me, as the leader, even what you don't do is noticed and can really affect your people in a positive or a negative way.

Working Mothers

All of the working mothers we had were ARs. The time and travel required of a CR probably wouldn't have worked very well for them, and we never had any ask to become a CR. I viewed having working mothers as a competitive advantage. I never gave them the double-take where we said one thing, but did another when it came to them taking time to manage working and raising children. Frankly, I felt lucky to have them, and I knew they realized juggling work and family would not be as easy elsewhere, so they were very loyal. This principle applied to my other people as well. I never really worried too much if they were taking time to coach a team or for their personal lives. We had a lot of children in our extended BMI family, and I understood spending the time. After all, it was what I did.

Knowing Your People

I really knew my people. I knew their backgrounds, their families and where they were from. I knew their story. I knew them well enough to tease them or give them a hard time about something. That was always my standard. I had to know them well enough to do that. In 2000, we grew to almost 200 people and I could feel that connection start to slip away from me. We had grown too fast, and I didn't like how that felt. The Recession of 2001-2004 got our numbers down gradually through attrition and, when we grew again, we did it more slowly.

Trust Me

While we didn't lower commission levels, we certainly did things that affected territory and accounts, which could potentially impact compensation. That was tricky. One of the reasons I did the numbers was so I could show my people how any changes we were going to implement would have no impact or minimal impact on them. However, there were times when I simply had to ask them to trust me. I was well aware I was making a commitment and that what I was telling them better happen and I made sure it did. I did not go out on this limb very often, but there were some key times with some key people when I did.

Recognition and Awards

A little known fact is that no organization in the world better at recognition programs than the U.S. military. They give medals and badges and coins and certificates for everything. All you have to do is look at the uniform and see what I mean. Not having a standard uniform in the civilian world that is easily recognizable makes this a lot tougher. However, we did our best. We gave out certificates and trophies, and recognized our long-termers with a Rolex watch for their 10th anniversary. We gave out plaques for our highest awards and made them really special. On each plaque we inscribed a fairly long paragraph, similar to a military citation, telling what the person had accomplished to earn the award.

Incentives

My take on incentives is that recognition makes more of a difference than the monetary amount. Problems occur when you don't update or change them. Keeping incentives the same for a long period of time begins to make them feel like compensation, which then causes problems when you attempt to change them. A few of our incentives stayed the same, but many did not. The trick was to change the incentives so they were not written in stone and taken for granted and became expected.

Company Trip

While we had bonuses for performance, the bulk of the compensation came from commissions. Additionally, we always went on a big company trip. We did this in a significantly different way from how other companies typically do it. Most companies have the top 10-20 percent (or less) of their salesforce be awarded a trip for top sales performance. In our company, only the bottom 10-20 percent did NOT go, and we always went as a group, often with as many as 150 people going. There was a minimum amount of time somebody had to be with the company, but we made the goal a company-wide goal. If the company achieved it, we went. If we didn't reach our goal, no one took a trip. This also had the side benefit of ensuring the trip was already funded. We ALWAYS went on the incentive trip.

We always made the goal reasonable and we always achieved it. Our people were able to bring a guest, and Sandy always did a remarkable job of finding great places for us to go. We went to Mexico, Key West, Las Vegas, The Bahamas, Jamaica, and on a couple of Caribbean cruises. As our ARs and CRs were sending companies and candidates to HCs around the country, it was crucial they have relationships with their mates in the other offices. These trips really developed those relationships and served as a lubricant for the future. We always had group activities on our trips, which included skits, beach Olympics, and basketball games, as well as formal events where our major awards were presented. These trips also gave the spouses a chance to get to know us and us them.

Meeting Parents

Whenever I had the chance to meet the parents of my people, I always dropped whatever I was doing and made a big deal out of it. I made sure to communicate how much their son or daughter was appreciated. This was an opportunity that wasn't going to come again, and I wanted to nail it. I remember Rear Admiral Mitchell doing that for me with my dad and I never forgot it. Whenever my people received our top awards, I always called their parents. (I also never forget that my boss at TLG, Carol Rifkin, had done this for me, when I was named Recruiter of the Year.)

Often it was the only time I ever spoke to them. Telling someone's parents their son or daughter had done something great was always fun and made a real difference to them. Few things are as enjoyable as making somebody look good in their parents' eyes. This was easy and fun. In the same vein as the handwritten notes, this was a small thing that was extra. I know it made a difference to my people, that I cared enough about them to do it.

The Initial Interview

Leadership is all about the connection, which begins with the first interview. It typically doesn't take very long to determine if you want the candidate. What are you doing to not only sell the opportunity, but to also make the connection? The messages you send set the table for your follow-on relationship. Are you intimidating? Do you smile? Are you interested in their personal story? When did your interview take place? If I did a phone interview, I often did it on the weekend or at night. Sometimes I did them on vacation. I wanted to send the message that I was always on the clock, and if they came to BMI, they had better be able to keep up with me.

Recognition for People Leaving the Company

I think it's important, when people who have been significant to the company leave, that there is recognition of what they meant to the group and a thank you for their efforts. Typically, a luncheon suffices. Besides the message to the person leaving, a powerful message is also communicated to those remaining with the company; this person meant something to us, just as you mean something to us, too.

Calls with My People

One of the things I was really committed to was talking with my people, all of the time. I never scheduled calls. I often called them just to say "hello". I genuinely liked them and, often, our conversation didn't even center on the business. We would talk about sports, their families, my family or tell stories. Of course, the business was talked about, but it was natural. Because they knew me well, they knew what my take would be on an issue. Consequently, they would make many decisions without even consulting me. I knew we had reached a high level when I started to hear my sayings and thoughts repeated back to me, oftentimes teasing me in the process.

Relationships are not created under stress. When you really need that relationship is not the time to build it. With 100+ people in our company, I began to notice I was talking to the same people all of the time, and I was missing others. To remedy this, I started using the company phone directory as a checklist to make sure I spoke to every person in the company at least once every quarter.

It was even better when I could call my people to tell them they did a great job. I always wanted my managers to send me the nuggets when their people did something well. I would then call that person and tell them their manager was bragging about them to me. This was unbelievably powerful stuff. The person knew their manager was looking out for them by telling me good things about them, and I was able to recognize them personally. Taking this a step further, whenever I got the chance, I would talk to their husband or wife, and tell them what a great job their spouse was doing. This made both parties feel great and appreciative in a way that almost has no equal.

Confrontation

I struggled internally when I had to deal with issues involving my direct reports and immediate support staff. I don't know if they ever felt my anxiety, but my personal connection with them was very important to me, and I didn't want to do anything to damage it. As often as I could, I tried to have them identify their own issue and solve it themselves. I tried to have the situation be the bad guy and not make it personal. When I did have to tackle an issue head-on, I girded my loins and dealt with it directly and succinctly, but it was never easy. Sugarcoating the issue wasn't going to make it any better or easier, so I didn't try.

Influence Without Management

There is a dynamic, especially with senior people who, while not in an official leadership position, have great influence. Most want to be able to affect things, without having the hassle of being in management. In our company, these people were the senior ARs, who carried tremendous weight, because their opinions and support mattered. All of them had access to me, and I asked for their opinion on almost anything we were considering.

Veto Power Over Hires

Tina Murphy was my office manager at TLG. I was very close to her, and was almost a father figure, especially after her father died. I did not take her with me when I left TLG because I wasn't sure what I was going to do and didn't want the responsibility for her leaving her present position, if whatever I ended up doing didn't work out. After about a year, she came onboard as our office manager. (One future day, she would become a very fine AR – the only office manager to ever make that leap). We had hired a few people who didn't work out and who Tina had reservations about before they were hired. Apparently, they behaved one way with us and another way with her. She had seen what they were really like. We ended up giving her virtual veto power over anyone we were considering hiring, even if we liked them. It made her feel good and protected us from ourselves.

Executive Steering Committee (ESC)

Because the leadership of BMI was so CR heavy, we created an ESC comprised of one AR from each office, who was elected by their peers. This gave them recognition and a voice on the various issues affecting the ARs. This also served to provide leadership opportunities for some of our senior ARs. While this was not nearly the same level of responsibility as running an HC or leading a branch or region, it was still significant and it mattered to them.

Just Say It

We've all heard stories of the father who doesn't show emotion or tell his children he loves them. Then the kids then grow up wishing they had heard the words. Your people aren't any different. Some leaders throw around compliments like manhole covers. Sometimes the person in charge thinks people are getting paid for doing their job, and that should be enough. Your people are starving to hear the words. Tell them you value them; tell them they are doing a good job; tell them something. Just say it!

One Placement Rule

Our rule was that a person could offer any input or suggestions, AFTER they made one placement. Obviously, we had a few people who, in addition to not making it, were major distractions by being pretty verbal about "improving" our system, well before they knew what they were talking about or what they were doing. This rule squashed much of that problem.

Giving Speeches

I found one way to practice public speaking was to volunteer to speak at the luncheons of local service organizations. There is someone in every organization who is responsible for lining up a speaker. You are making that person's day by calling them and volunteering to be a speaker as they now don't have to worry about getting one. I gave speeches to Kiwanis, Optimist, and Rotary groups, and it was very easy. However, one of the things that made me uncomfortable was when they read my bio when introducing me. Getting an impressive bio on your website or in your literature is important, but having it read to a group in front of you is awkward. Sometimes, when I got up in front of the group to speak, I felt like saying, "Well, Shaun Bradley couldn't be here today, so he sent me."

Sunday Night Calls

As we had HCs nearly every Sunday/Monday of the year, in locations around the country, I obviously couldn't be at all of them and didn't need to be. However, I always wanted a report from the CCs on Sunday night, to let me know how everything went during the first day of the HC. This served a couple of purposes. First, I just wanted to know how things had gone, as that event was a big deal and how we made much of our money. Besides, I would be going crazy if I didn't know. Second, it sent a message to my people there that they were important enough for me to want to hear from them on a Sunday.

Bad News

Bad news doesn't get better. I always wanted to know bad news right away. The fastest way to not know what was going on was to take bad news poorly. Shooting the messenger ensured you wouldn't get any future messages. Sometimes I would get these calls at home at night. I always was glad I got the call, even if the issue wasn't that serious. I always thanked that person for calling, me because I wanted my people to feel they weren't imposing on me, as the one time they might hesitate, would be the one time I really needed to know.

Need to Listen

Most people have an almost primal need for you to listen to them. This is not to be confused with you agreeing with them, or even doing what they want you to do. Just listening makes them feel valued and, in most cases, they will appreciate the fact you considered what they had to say, to be enough.

Taking Compliments Well

A lot of good people are really bad at this. They will often deflect the credit or say it wasn't that big of a deal. This may be well intentioned, but has the effect of making the person giving the compliment feel uncomfortable. I would tell my people who did this to just be gracious, say "thank you" and shut up. I explained that their attempt to be humble was denying the person giving the compliment the opportunity to feel good about giving them one.

Oreo Effect

The human psyche is much more open to hearing something negative only AFTER hearing something positive. You can pretty much say anything to anyone if you start with how much you love them but...and and finish with how much you love them. I called this the Oreo effect. I tended to be pretty positive in what I said to people, but it was also important my words have credibility by noting things that weren't done well or correctly. Another technique I used for emphasis was saying, "Just so you know I wasn't blowing smoke when I told you how great the last job you did was, this isn't one of them."

Introducing My People

Whenever I introduced one of my people, I ALWAYS said we worked together. I NEVER said they worked for me.

Good News

Whenever we had good news to deliver, whether it was for a promotion, a good collection, a surprise, or whatever, we seldom sat on it. We made it a habit to enjoy it immediately, and shared the excitement for as long as possible. There were certainly enough tough things that would happen that were not pleasant and they would happen soon enough.

Moral Authority

When I left TLG, I had a non-solicitation agreement. While these things are often said to be unenforceable, nonetheless I had signed it. Prior to BMI opening our doors, I visited Art Lucas to tell him what we were going to do. I know he appreciated and respected hearing it in person, directly from me. He wished me luck and said we were good, as long as I didn't go after the already established TLG clients for a year. I told him, "Of course, I wouldn't."

Even with a good like Art, too much was on the line if he challenged us, or if one of my people, even by mistake, went after a client TLG had. TLG had a database of military units and billets with corresponding addresses to send mailers to potential candidates advertising their services. I spoke with one of TLG managers and arranged to buy it. I had created that list while I was there and could have very easily created our own. But, TLG cashing our check put them in bed with us, so if there ever was a problem down the road, we would be protected.

For the first year, our people knew what companies they could not call. The power of this cannot be overstated. Our people knew why that list existed. For us to not go after any of those companies sent a message that could not have been communicated any other way. Our people knew we did things right. We made the hard right decision when it hurt. I truly believe there were few things we ever did that were more important. In business, your own people know if you're clean or not. There were a few times when things happened, that from a distance could have been misunderstood, and I did not have the luxury of providing the details to my people. All I had to rely on was my word and the history that we had always done things the right way. This was always good enough for my people.

Buying Lunch For People

This might not seem like a big deal, but it's the day-to-day things that are the landmines, and this was tricky. I often ate lunch with my people, but resisted the urge to pick up the tab. If I did it a few times, then it would become expected. Then, if I didn't, it could cause some awkwardness. The flip side of this was that sometimes I felt I should pick it up, as I was the boss. I settled for up picking up the tab for the person having the anniversary or luncheon in their honor, as well as for the CR lunch the day before the HC, since everyone was going to be working late.

Messages Without Words

Powerful messages are often communicated, without even saying a word. Your people will watch your relationship with your family. There is an opportunity to include your family by having them come to the office, and by your spouse being visible and supportive. How she treated your people had a direct effect on how you were perceived. Fair or not, your people watched everything you did. They noticed what you wore, what you drove, where you parked, what you were good at and, more importantly, what you didn't do well.

Going in Early

The recession of 2001-2004 was brutal. I knew my people had bet their future and their family's future on me, and I could not let them down. During that period, I also came to know a truism of business – sometimes there is only so much you can do, and you just have to endure and tough it out. There were times when I knew yesterday was bad, today was awful and tomorrow was going to be worse than today. Sales fell by 60 percent. No company endures that without trauma. And while I thought I knew what tough was, having started BMI during the recession of 1991-1992, I learned that was only the warm-up.

During mid-2003, I went to my wife and told her that we had had a good run and our life was pretty sweet, but some things were about to change. I felt like we were doing everything we could to get through this awful recession, and I didn't know what else to do, so I told her that for the foreseeable future, I would be waking up at 4 a.m. and getting into the office before 5 a.m. I truly didn't know if it would make any difference and, to be honest, I still don't. But I was determined to set the best possible example and maybe that would motivate my people to dig in even more and work even harder. I did this until mid-2004, and it almost killed me, but we came out of the crisis intact.

Never Delegate the Hard Decisions

The dirtiest and messiest decisions could NEVER be delegated. YOU had to do them personally. This trained your people on how to do them, and also sent a message that when the going got rough you led from the front.

Tolerating Inappropriate Behavior

Never tolerate even innocent wayward comments. In my experience, really good people can say some really stupid things. Most of the time, it came in the form of a joke told to a group or in email. While I personally believe in the principle of "praise in public and reprimand in private," this was the exception. My rule was always to hammer the person in front of the group who had heard the offensive words, or as a reply-all to the email. When I could, I always gave the offending person notice in private about what was about to happen. I met with them or called them and told them what they had done was unacceptable and, while I knew they were a good person, this was not OK. I told them I had a responsibility to BMI to make sure everybody knew I didn't think what they had done was OK, so they were about to get reprimanded in a very public way. I never got pushback, and they were always contrite and, more importantly, it never happened again.

This sent a message that might have been among the most powerful I ever sent. I always felt like I was protecting the minority part of the group. You never really know the full details of people's background, and the fastest way to destroy a team is to make people feel excluded or marginalized from it. Whether the comment or joke was about sexual orientation or religion or race, it was a cancer that was easy to prevent if you paid attention to it. We were loose and informal with many things, but never with this.

We also had a situation where one of our male employees was being physically inappropriate with one of our female employees. We quickly determined the complaint was legitimate, and he was fired that day. I called Security in advance of doing this, just in case there was a problem. Later on, there were some oddities with this same person, when he found employment at another recruiting firm (non-military), and dressed up like a hotel worker to go through our trash after an HC to get the brief sheets and the leads those would generate. Six months later, I saw this same person walking towards me at the opposite end of the 10th floor of an Atlanta hotel. We were the only ones on that floor, and I was concerned, as I thought he might attack me, but he walked by without incident.

Client Relationships - Honesty

When something went wrong with a client, there was always a tendency to hope the client didn't find out. Bad move. As long as honest mistakes didn't happen too often, they respected and trusted you for being upfront and truthful with them. Tell them, tell them immediately, and be frank with them. Tell them where you screwed up and how you will make it up to them. Clients don't expect perfection, because they're not perfect either. They will respect and trust you, if you own up to your mistakes. Besides, they're going to find out eventually, so you might as well try to make points with them.

When I was working both the client and candidate side at TLG, one of my clients was GE Capital and I sent Eddie Meyers, USNA '82 and a former Atlanta Falcons running back, on an interview after his playing days were over. The position was in Nashville, but the interview was at corporate in Charlotte. I gave Eddie detailed information with directions from the airport to where he was to interview. Eddie called me after leaving the airport in a rental car to say he could not find any of the streets or highways on the directions I had given him. I immediately knew I had really messed up and had mistakenly sent him to Nashville. I knew I had to take the bullet on this; it wasn't Eddie's fault and I didn't want my mistake to reflect on him. I called my client and immediately told him what happened and said this was totally my fault and apologized. He was good about it, and Eddie got back on a plane, flew to Charlotte, and eventually landed the position.

I Ate Last

Whenever there was a potluck lunch, I consciously always ate last. Whenever we flew on our company trips, my wife and I boarded last (to my wife's chagrin). If I ever had a first class upgrade when I was flying with any of my people, I always had them use it. These were small things, but I was constantly aware of the little messages I could send. Some people noticed these things and word got around.

No Favorites

While my relationship with each person was different, as they were different people, any real or perceived favoritism on my part would have been a cancer. In other words, all of the brothers or sisters had to feel I loved them all the same. This meant I had to deny myself some fun experiences. I had common interests with some of them, but not all, and I had to be very careful about not sending the message that I liked some more than others.

While I worked predominantly out of Atlanta, with offices around the country, I took every precaution to make sure there was no perceived favoritism when decisions were made. The people in Atlanta simply had better access to me by virtue of their proximity. If all other things were equal, I always gave the nod to the non-Atlanta operation.

The Light of Day

You could never make a decision that would not stand the light of day. Many decisions needed to stay private. But our standard was if the decision became public, it could be defended, and there were sound reasons why the decision was made.

Bio

Be careful with this. Stories abound of people who got into trouble by exaggerating their resume, and when it caught up with them, their world came crashing down. George O'Leary lost the Notre Dame Head Coaching job because he allowed his bio to say he had lettered in football at the University of New Hampshire, when he had not. I was a recruited football player at Navy and played my freshman year and freshman season; however, after suffering three major leg injuries in the scope of 17 months (two at USNA, after my injury in high school), I gave up football. I never earned a varsity letter in college and I knew had I even put football anywhere on my bio, soon enough it could have been embellished one way or another. I then would have to spend time correcting the error, which would have been awkward. I also was uncomfortable with the potential of being given credit for earning the varsity letter my classmates had been awarded, so I eliminated that possibility.

Not Being Showy

I was always conscious of being showy in front of my people. I think people want to know their leaders are successful, but they don't want it waved in their faces to remind them of what they don't have. When BMI was minting money, I bought my wife an emerald necklace that was encased in diamonds. This was easily the nicest thing I'd ever bought before or since. While she wore it on other occasions, she would never wear it to company functions.

Romantic Relationships in the Office

As somebody who lived this, I suppose my viewpoint is somewhat jaded, but I think these situations are inevitable. Human nature is human nature. Our experiences ran the gamut. We had the very positive experience of people meeting at BMI and then getting married. We also had already married people develop an extra-marital affair, which ended in divorce and our losing both of them. I think the line is crossed when it is a direct report situation or when one of the involved party can influence or impact the career of the other.

People Working Remotely

We tried doing this a number of times, with only a single success story. We actually hired people to work in Germany and on Okinawa, Japan, to recruit the candidates who were stationed there. We also had a few people we thought were good enough to work in our offices initially, with plans for them to eventually work remotely. None of these were ever successful. The only success we had with somebody working remotely was when one of our early superstars, Beth Jarvis, moved to Washington, DC, and worked out of her home. The difference was Beth was well established, and had years working closely with the people in the Atlanta office, as well as with her peers nationally. She knew and trusted them, and they felt the same towards her. Our office environment, and the relationships that engendered, was just too crucial to our operation for people who weren't physically connected to make it go. It also takes a unique personality to work independently without daily interaction with their peers.

Earn It First

I learned the hard way to make people earn or deserve it, before they were given the golden nuggets that would almost always lead to placements. Whether this was assigning candidates, who were already locked in to attend an HC, or providing a call-in lead for a company that wanted to hire military candidates, giving these golden nuggets to those who hadn't earned it yet was a bad idea. Despite the best intentions of helping, people valued what they earned and did themselves. Only after they had done things the hard way did they truly appreciate a helping hand.

Punctuality

I was always obsessive about being places early. I'm sure this stems from my Navy days, when I was so worried about oversleeping and missing ship's movement that I always slept onboard the ship the night before we left port. There was no excuse, especially for an officer, to ever be late. My kids heard "losers are late" more often than they care to remember.

Inspect Versus Expect

As I mentioned earlier, we provided candidates with a written brief on every company they would interview at our HCs. These were not only important for the information provided to the candidate, but also were a reflection of the professionalism of our people. Military people are well educated and will judge, sometimes harshly, a person by the quality of their writing skills. As our ARs needed to sell their client opportunities to the candidates, they started from behind if their brief sheet was not first-rate.

While there was a format for the way these were written, their quality was all over the map and it drove me nuts. (Once the son of a proofreader, always the son of a proofreader.) After a few failed attempts to see some improvement, I decided the only way to get them where I wanted was to personally grade and correct every brief sheet for every HC. I did that for about a year. My people then knew I would review them so they improved dramatically. However, there were still some people who just had poor writing skills, despite being college graduates. I went to the people whose brief sheets were literally works of art and who were recognized as the best in the company. I asked them, as a favor to me, to help their mates by showing them how to write one and reviewing their peer's brief sheets before the HC. What was interesting was a couple of our best had not finished college. While the people who needed the help never got to the level of the stars, their brief sheets became passable, and the stars were recognized by me, for excelling at something that previously had not been highlighted.

Speed of Decision

One of the areas where we really excelled was speed of decision making. If we had the money, and both Sandy and I agreed on it, we were fearless in making a decision, and our confidence grew as most of what we were doing was working. After placing only officer candidates since we opened, we made the huge and game-changing decision to start recruiting, and placing Enlisted candidates in 30 minutes over lunch. No kidding.

Gifts from Vendors

It was a little thing, but I often gave gift items from our vendors to our office support people. These gifts were generally not significant money-wise, although some were for dinners at nice restaurants. However, the simple gesture of you receiving something, and then giving it to somebody who is supporting you, makes an impression.

Ideas

If you want people to come up with ideas, you have to encourage them and ensure people know bad ideas are valued, too. At least the person had the initiative to suggest something. To encourage this, I would tell people my bad idea story. One of our offices was in the North Atlanta suburbs, and I hoped we could recruit mothers who were ready to re-enter the workforce, as we had great success with them. I thought a great place to run a recruiting ad would be in one of the local AMC 24 movie theaters. We created an ad I thought looked pretty good, and it ran in every movie, every day for a month. Probably 20,000 people saw our ad. I would typically ask the people hearing this story how many people they thought responded to the ad. I would always get an answer like 50 or 100. When I said, "One," it always brought a lot of laughter, and certainly sent the message that it was OK if they had an idea that didn't work out.

I almost never saw the really great ideas figured out by sitting around a conference table. They tend to be found by immersion in the nitty-gritty and the muck, and, in the process, modifying them as you went along. The best ideas are always the simple ones. I think the reason is that more complex ideas may be better on paper, but in execution and explanation, they fail because they just have too many moving parts.

The Ones You Start With

Unfortunately, for the most part, the people you start with are not always the ones who finish or even last long term. Talent is upgraded over time, and not everyone who was good enough at the beginning has the ability to grow as the company grows.

Mess Decks

One of the primary responsibilities of the Supply Department onboard an aircraft carrier is to feed the crew. While we were in our homeport near San Francisco, our ship was having issues in this area - long lines, dirty utensils, and cold food. The basics weren't getting done. (On a Navy ship if the food ain't right, ain't nothin' right!) Our next deployment wasn't scheduled for another 12 months. As the Aviation Supply Officer, my division was doing the preparatory work to be ready. However, as the air wing my group supported was back at their home air stations and off of our ship, I was available for other duties. Rear Admiral (then Commander) Mitchell pulled me out of my area and sent me to fix the Mess Decks (where the crew ate and the food was prepared).

First, I identified the real leaders and talent. Unfortunately, it wasn't the more senior leadership, which was one of the reasons there were issues to begin with. There were stars among the young watch captains, who prepared the food and had been doing a great job in their specific areas of responsibility. I moved them into leadership positions even though they were only 22 to 23 years old. The quality of all the food improved immediately. I found someone to fix the dishwashers, so the utensils were clean. I then went around and asked the crew while they were eating if the food was OK. That had not been done before.

There were limits on how we could fix the long lines. However, I had been receiving USA Today in the mail, so I had news the crew wasn't getting. We had an electronic tickertape positioned where the crew could view the various ship announcements while in the food line. We decided to put the sports news from my newspaper on the tickertape each day. The time in the lines didn't decrease, but because the crew was reading news of interest to occupy their time while they waited, it made the lines seem shorter. It was an awesome experience. I learned it was always about the talent. Experience is overrated. Motivated talent always wins out.

Letting Go and Delegating

Delegating wasn't hard for me to do, which I think made me a bit unique as an entrepreneur. I knew how good my people were, and I liked having them involved. I also think you insult high achievers when you don't let them run with the things they are capable of doing. There were often times when I thought they probably did things better than I would have done them anyhow. There were only a couple of things, such as doing the numbers and managing the mailout database, that I never delegated, as I felt I needed to maintain personal control over them.

Fundamentals of Good Leaders

Most solid families pretty much function the same way, and dysfunctional ones seem to all be messed up, but all in different ways. I think the same can be said of companies and organizations. Having been in a number of different arenas in my life, I can say good leadership is pretty much the same regardless of fields. Whether it is in the military, coaching, as a father, or in business, the building blocks of leadership are the same; being worthy of trust, caring about your people, and getting the job done; it is always doing those fundamentals that makes things work. Good leaders come in all different sizes and shapes, but doing those three things are common to all of them. I think the trick is to do all three. Failing to do even one of the three building blocks makes the others irrelevant. You will fail as a leader, if you don't do them all.

Real leadership requires a willingness to sacrifice for others. This may seem counterintuitive in a capitalist system, but your people have to know you will look out for them. They don't expect their leader to be Saint Francis of Assisi, but they have to know, if it came down to it, you were willing to sacrifice something of your own for them. It didn't really matter if it was time, money, credit, territory, vacation days, or opportunity didn't really matter. What did make the difference was knowing you cared enough to sacrifice something that mattered to you for them.

Military Leadership in a Civilian World

The stereotype people have of military leadership has always amazed me. What I saw during my years of active duty was relentlessly positive leadership. While I'm sure it happened, outside of Plebe Summer at the Naval Academy, I would have to think long and hard to remember anybody yelling or screaming. Successful leaders in the military served as coaches and teachers. Unfortunately, many civilians conjure up an image of strict, no-nonsense, rigid authoritarians. Just like any easily identifiable group, individuals can certainly be found to validate that stereotype. However, anyone who thought that, and then observed us at BMI, would have been stunned. We were loose, had fun, and got the job done. All types and styles were welcome.

F to D

There were times I talked to my senior managers when they had a big problem or issue, and I could tell they thought it was just too hard to fix. I needed them to believe they could do it. Sometimes their morale was just beaten down by their sense of failure. They needed to feel some success. I often told them, "Let's go from an F to a D. If we can do that, we'll get 100 percent improvement, and then we'll go from there." This also served to let them know I recognized the scope of the problem, and wasn't expecting miracles overnight, but rather for them to just make things a bit better and then build on that.

Money as a Weapon

There are few more built-in conflicts than how people are paid. If you can get people to take less, then in theory you make more. As much as possible, I liked pay systems that rewarded performance. The more they did, the more money they made, the more the company made, and then we were all moving in the same direction. When you decided their pay, you were also making a statement as to their worth, which could be very subjective and lead to a lot of negative feelings. The more objective the criteria for pay, and the more control THEY had to determine their own paycheck, the better for all. The real trick was connecting pay to what you needed done. We needed placements, so that was what our people were paid for making. We paid a bonus for things like having a certain number of companies or certain types of candidates attending an HC, because those building blocks led to placements.

Systems with Legs

Systems or programs that were not self-sustaining used to drive me crazy. Almost always they were big ideas that answered some "flavor of the day" problem. Everyone became excited about the new thing and then, six months later, the new system or program didn't even exist.

Ongoing training was a classic example of this. Too many times, training got done one time. Then the immediate issues of the day became the priority, which caused the next training time to be cancelled. Soon enough, the training was totally forgotten. What I have seen be successful were smaller programs that were simple to execute. There also needed to be a champion, who believed in the new program and who would make sure it was actually implemented. Our Aftercare program was a good example of this.

Daily Call Monitoring

We tried daily call monitoring but, to be honest, my heart wasn't in it. It wasn't implemented well and didn't have legs. The technology was not good, and my sense was our people should have been motivated enough and good enough to not need it. Monitoring the number of calls they made was a very blunt instrument, and not always a good indicator of what they were doing, anyhow. Who our people were talking to and what they were saying mattered a lot more. Great people bristle at this kind of micromanaging. I know I would have. Besides, I simply didn't have the aptitude to be worried about how many individual calls people were making, and didn't like being around people who needed that much close supervision. I wanted to respect my people, and babysitting them wasn't part of the deal.

Confident Doesn't Mean Correct

There can be a tendency to listen more to the person who is the most passionate, enthusiastic or confident. People who were that sure of themselves, or of their opinion, always made me a bit wary. In our world, I was truly a subject matter expert, and much of the time even I wasn't sure what to do. How could they be so sure? There was almost always another way to do it, or some risk was involved in any decision, and I always wanted those to at least be weighed or considered.

Implementing Change

If you had to make a change, make sure you went all the way. It hurts just as much to do it halfway, and if you stopped before you truly implemented the change, you then had the worst of all worlds. You upset everybody with the change, and it wouldn't work. If you went down the change road, which wasn't easy, but sometimes necessary, at least complete your objective. For us, implementing RW, creating the ABAL and establishing new Disciplines were major things, to which we were committed. In each instance, there were challenges and pushback. We could have implemented them more easily, but if we had been less steadfast, then would not have had the great final results. Over time, as the key changes we made were successful, we became more confident in ourselves in making those changes, and we encountered a lot less resistance due to our previous successes.

Planning

I was not gifted administratively. So,I tracked all of the ongoing projects in a manila folder and highlighted them when completed. This enabled me to look at all of the projects I had going on at the same time. I also developed the habit of writing the daily things I needed to knock out in a spiral notebook and highlighting them once they were done. There were probably better ways to keep on track, but I kept all of these. In cleaning out my desk for the last time, I looked them over and reread the history of BMI. Both the manila folders and the spiral notebooks were invaluable in jogging my memory to accurately write this book.

I never believed too much in five-year plans, especially in a startup or a small business, as things changed too quickly. You had to get the initial idea and strategy right, or you'd pretty much sink. Beyond that, you needed to stay flexible. You had to focus on simultaneously living in worlds of today, next week, two months from now, six months from now, and next year. You had to pay attention to the future and survive for today. Because if you didn't plan for the future, the day when things got better would never come.

Rules Don't Apply Equally

Performers are given room and aren't treated the same as everyone else. Most people don't want to be micromanaged, but they need to earn that right. There was no question some people in our company had more influence or were treated differently, but it was because they were performers.

Pace of the Leader

No one cares, or should care, more than the person in charge. If talented people feel they care more than the person in charge, soon enough they will find a place where they will be well led, or they will end up taking the leader's job, as that person probably doesn't deserve it anyhow. My people knew I was all in, and the success of BMI determined the financial success of my family. I had no backup plan and my people knew it.

What If?

When I saw what happened on Wall Street in 2008, I knew the "What if?" question wasn't being asked very often, or the really bad scenarios weren't being considered. Maybe this was because many of the big firms were public companies, and weren't playing with their own money. All I know, is there were few days when I didn't ask myself that question. What if this person left? What if sales decreased by a certain percentage? What if there was a snowstorm and an HC was cancelled? What if Sandy got sick? What if there was a recession? Financially, it is recommended to have six months of cash in an emergency fund. I had six years of cash. I also knew my personal savings were the last line of defense for BMI.

My personal barometer was to imagine the worst-case scenario, then double it. If I would still be left standing if that happened, I was OK and could sleep well at night. I always wanted backups for backups for backups. I exhaled in 1997, after we had back-to-back good years in Atlanta and things were really solid, and then again in 2007, after we had survived the recession and had our best year ever. Other than those times, I always felt anxiety, but I learned to wear it, so it didn't infect others and affect my decisions. Having backups was one of the reasons we created the separate Disciplines, so we would not be solely dependent on any one of them. This was also a reason we brought in minority owners (more on that later), so we had some leadership flexibility along with committed bench strength.

Authenticity

I always felt pretty confident about my writing skills, but there were some other good writers in our company as well. I made a habit of including them, and asking their opinion on some of the things I wrote. Part of this was because I valued their opinions, and they made positive additions and corrections. It also helped build a bond with them knowing I thought highly of their skills. When we hired Bill Scott as our Director of Marketing, who had CNN experience, there was a time when I felt what he wrote sounded better or was more appropriate than what I had written. I was also guilty of thinking anyone who had that level of experience knew more about official communications than I did. After a few times using his words with my name attached to them, one of my people came up to me and said, "You didn't write that. We know it because it doesn't sound like you." After that, and while I valued his input, I wrote and used my own words. Authenticity matters.

My Name on Things

One thing I developed over the years was the confidence to not need to have my fingerprints on every single thing we did. It was fine if I didn't have anything to do with it and, in many cases, it was better. I learned it didn't matter who was the author or who got the credit, because if it worked, it had my name on it and if it didn't work, it had my name on it as well. It only mattered if it worked. There was a defining moment about this during our early years. We had promulgated a new medical and dental plan. Afterwards, one of our people came to us and said we were pretty much off base. He said he knew something about insurance plans, and was sure we could get a cheaper and better plan. After getting past our bruised egos, we checked into it and ended up going back to our people with new information and a better plan. This was a little embarrassing, but the end result was better, and that was what mattered.

Public Accountability

There are few things more potent than public accountability to the group. Sales charts were important. We also used grease boards, where a person's name was noted next to the name of the company they confirmed to attend the HC. The key was to make the boards visible, and ensure what was highlighted mattered. Tracking or highlighting everything just minimized what was really important. Performers wanted to know where they stood in the performance queue. In addition, new performance records needed to be highlighted and publicized. When I was at TLG, no one before me had ever billed $200K in a year. Within a year, other people were breaking that barrier, as they realized it could be done.

Firing People

Most of the time, I didn't have much angst about firing people. Some were people who I thought had given it a good go, but just didn't have the skills to get the job done. I always tried to let them know I thought they were a good person, who would do well somewhere, but just not here. I always tried to get them to resign. Another group was made up of people who either were problems or just didn't try very hard. In this case, I felt they fired themselves. While I would try to get them to resign, as it would be less disruptive, if they didn't seize the opportunity, I just fired them. Another category was made up of people who had done something egregious. Firing them sent a message to the rest of the company as to whether your policies really had teeth. Dishonesty and sexual harassment were situations where the person had to simply be fired. While you didn't need to make an announcement why you did what you did, everyone figured it out soon enough.

The roughest ones were people who had been promoted to management and just weren't doing the job, and their lack of performance was negatively affecting others in the company. They were typically good recruiters, but had failed as managers. Having them return to recruiting was not going to work for them or for us. We gave them a severance package, but in every case it was difficult.

Replacing a Manager

We were unbelievably careful with this situation. We never discussed the person who was going to be let go with their eventual replacement, although we knew ahead of time who we wanted it to be. We did not involve the new manager in any way. The two of them typically already had some sort of relationship, and we wanted the new manager to be free of any perceived involvement.

Definition of Success

While in the Navy, I discovered one of the things that drove me was the feeling of respect I received from the senior and junior enlisted on my ship but, in particular, from the senior enlisted. You could tell by the way they talked to you and looked at you, whether they respected you. That feeling was like a drug for me. Throughout my life, getting that feeling, whether from the kids I coached or my people at BMI, was of paramount importance to me. The money and recognition mattered, but nothing was as crucial to me as earning their respect. It affected everything I did and how I did it.

I always felt if I wasn't the best, or didn't have a plan to be the best, I was just wasting my time. This was really important to me. I always felt I had to at least have the possibility to be the best, or the group I was with did. While I know my people thought I set a good example, I always felt I had to be worthy to lead such great people. This meant I had to be able to look in the mirror, check myself, and believe I was worthy. This drove me more than expectations from anyone else.

Difficult People

Handling difficult people was one of the most trying of all the issues I faced. Since a lot of people in a recruiting firm tended to have unique personalities, it was a given that a few would be difficult. It would have been nice to address this by not hiring them, but some were going to slip through. Difficult people tended to be irritating and annoying. As long as they weren't in a leadership position, the damage they could do was limited, and they tended to isolate themselves anyway. However, if they were a producer, you had to manage them, try to bring them along, and minimize the problems they created. As good as we were and as much team chemistry as we had, we still had a few bad apples. I suppose in a business that is really people driven at every level, it was inevitable and it's remarkable we didn't have more.

Subject Matter Expert

You must be a subject matter expert in your business, and be perceived as such. Now, you still want to surround yourself with people who are smarter or more talented than you are. However, you must have an area where you are considered to be an expert. People will not listen or respect somebody who is not good at what they do. Coming from an aircraft carrier, I viewed leadership in a recruiting firm as very similar to being Commanding Officer (CO) of an aviation squadron. The CO had to be a good leader and a great pilot or a great leader and a good pilot. Being good at both was not enough, as the pilots being led would not respond if it wasn't some combination of good and great. Recruiting is a frontline business. Recruiters, whose very income is on the line, simply won't follow a leader who doesn't have credibility. Being a good recruiter and a great leader, or vice versa, was almost mandatory for leadership success. Being great at both was the ideal, but few met that standard.

A Troubled Group

How do you deal with a group that had problems? Gutting the operation would only make matters worse, as then you had no capability. There were times when the axiom "addition by subtraction" applied, but you couldn't do that en masse, as you still needed people to do the work. Oftentimes there was a new manager in place who needed encouragement more than anything else. The key was getting the right people on the team. Once I knew things were moving in the right direction, I told my managers the tide would be turned when those who "got it" outnumbered those who didn't.

Shaun G. Bradley

CHAPTER 11

Ethical
and
Operating Principles

Consistency in decision-making is really important. People need to understand and respect how and why decisions are made. We developed a set of principles to guide us in making decisions. We felt every decision should fall under either an ethical or an operating principle.

These were not always easy to ferret out. Sometimes there were competing goals and situations, but the sheer process of sorting through them helped us to identify the underlying principles, and then highlight them to our people. When we wrestled with an issue, we almost always did it as a group, so our people, or at least our managers, would have input. This also allowed them to see the angst we felt about the issue. They could understand how and why a decision was made, and what principle helped us make that decision. They could then explain to their people why a decision was made and, more importantly, make the decision on their own in the future, because they understood the philosophy behind the decision-making process. When we made a precedent-setting decision, we were very careful to project the underlying principle onto similar situations that might come up in the future, to ensure we had thought things through. While the list that follows is not comprehensive, it does provide an overview of some of the principles under which we operated.

We NEVER encouraged anyone to leave the military. If candidates asked us why they should leave the service, we told them they shouldn't. Everybody eventually leaves the service, and it was simply impossible to compare a military job and career to that of a civilian. We provided information on what was available to them in the civilian world, and helped them make an informed decision on what to do. Some of our candidates decided to stay in the service, but if they did, they made a positive decision to do so. In our minds, this was better for both them and the service. Most people who leave the military do so for reasons all having to do with the military (more time with family, too many deployments, want to do something else), not because they were lured away by the civilian world. As many of us were veterans, it also didn't seem right to convince someone to leave. Besides, we didn't need to do it. There were already plenty of candidates getting out every year.

We never bad-mouthed a competitor. I believed in the John Wooden philosophy, where he didn't spend much, if any, time scouting his basketball opponents. His philosophy was to make UCLA as good as they could possibly be. If they did what they were supposed to do, they would win independent of what their opponent did. For us, it was the same. When we lost a client, a placement or a candidate, it was almost always because of what we didn't do, or what we did to ourselves. Maybe we were outhustled or we didn't read it right or we squandered our opportunity. Besides, when you throw mud you just get some on yourself. Speaking poorly of a competitor risked alienating whoever you were talking to. You didn't know their history, or if they had a prior relationship with that company. In general, if we had a competitor doing unprofessional things, it just hurt our ability to sell the concept of hiring military candidates at all. Speaking poorly of them would only make matters worse.

When our ARs would learn that prospective clients were using a competitor and were happy with the service they were getting, we would tell them we wanted to be in the "on-deck circle" and, hopefully, get a chance to earn their business. We told them we were glad they had seen the value of hiring military. That was at least one battle we wouldn't have to fight. I remember when I entered our business and people, who didn't even know me, bad-mouthed me and the company I worked for (TLG). It was a habit for them. I was so new I couldn't have done anything to negatively impact them. In fact, I was so new, I hadn't done anything at all. I literally wasn't even in a position to compete with them, but criticizing competitors was just how they did business. I vowed, if I was ever in a position to be an industry leader, I would be different.

Among the first things I always told new hires in training was we never bad-mouthed a competitor. Reasons for this were many, but as a company principle, I believed it was the bastion of the weak to sell from a position of what the other company couldn't do, instead of talking about what we could do. I also felt saying negative things externally about a competitor could become a habit that would lead to saying negative things internally about each other. I also made the effort, once I was in the position of being an industry leader, to welcome new competitors when they were first starting. This ensured my first conversation with them would not be to discuss a problem or an issue. If there ever was an issue, my previous call almost always helped the issue to be resolved more easily.

Once you're an industry leader, you can help shape your entire industry by the example of how you conduct business. You still want to beat your competition, but you also want to have relationships with them. Bad actors in your industry tend to give the entire industry a bad name. While they hurt themselves, they also create inefficiencies that waste a good company's time. The joint ventures we did with some of our competitors would never have happened, had there not been an environment of trust created. If you're lucky, you will have competition you respect. And when you lose, it will be because of what YOU didn't do, not what they did to you.

We eventually acquired one of our competitors and, while you always hear horror stories about acquisitions, this one went flawlessly. The biggest reasons were our values were in line, and we had never spoken poorly about each other. We also received untold numbers of referrals over the years from our competition, as we were perceived as the ethical good guys.

We actually had an annual full-contact flag football game against our chief competition (TLG). When I say full contact, I'm not exaggerating. There were many former college athletes, and even a former NFL lineman who played. We had referees, lined fields, and special rules. It was called the DogBone Bowl. This was a big deal. A trophy was created, on which was inscribed the winner and final score of every game played. It was proudly displayed for the following year in the lobby of the winning company. People flew into Atlanta from all over the country for this game. Post-game parties were held. A total of seven games were played before age, injuries, and common sense prevailed, and it was shelved. It pains me to write this, but TLG won four of the seven games, including the finale to take permanent possession of the trophy.

We did not play God with convincing a candidate to take a job. Now that doesn't mean we didn't sell our opportunities hard, but we never withheld information or told candidates things that weren't true. Sometimes we had internally competing offers, where one fee was higher than the other. We NEVER allowed the size of the fee to enter into our thought process on what to do. NEVER.

We also made the decision to never recruit candidates away from the company where we had placed them, unless the client gave us permission to do so. Our rules were very strict with this. We required the candidates to notify their current employer that they wanted to work with us to help them find a new job, and then the client had to tell us it was OK. Obviously this served as a deterrent for the candidates to not work with us and most simply called one of our competitors. It just didn't seem right for us to place candidates into a company's front door, only to take them out of those same company's back door to place them again. We held fast to this principle, even if the client was no longer using us.

We were loyal to the ARs who had broken an account, to ensure they would reap the maximum benefit from having established that relationship, even when it hurt our ability to maximize the number of placements we might have made. The classic thought in Corporate America, to maximize sales with any client or territory is, if one person can produce X, then three people working that same area can produce three times X. We never did that. Loyalty to the original AR who created the relationship mattered to us.

We would only work with candidates who had received an Honorable Discharge. This seems like a pretty easy thing to do, as a candidate who had issues in the military would probably have follow-on issues in the civilian world. However, there were some pretty good people who made some bad decisions or did some unfortunate things, that caused us to want to help them. But our principle protected us from ourselves.

We erred on the side of the person or company that had actually done the work. In our industry, there was a tendency to "shotgun" resumes into companies, resulting in the submitted resume being marked for whatever firm sent it in. They hoped to be get the placement credit and corresponding fee, regardless of how a placement eventually occurred. The problem is thousands of resumes sit in companies' internal systems without any action being taken on them. In general, the initial interview is the key to the placement eventually happening. This was not a universally held view, but it was ours. Obviously, this could cause problems, and clients hated getting involved in this type of dispute. We felt the "but for" rule should apply. This means, "but for" the initial interview occurring, the placement would not have happened, and whatever firm made that interview happen should be given the placement credit. There were times when my own people had "shotgunned" a resume into a client, and to their dismay, I gave the placement credit to the other firm that had done the work by setting up the initial interview.

There were other principles which guided us to be sure, but underlying all of them was doing the right thing. I can honestly say I never felt, even for one day during my time at BMI, that we had done anything slimy or shady, or didn't feel OK. I could look at my people and have them look at me, and there was a great feeling of pride in how we had conducted our business.

CHAPTER 12

Selling Military

Our sales force was often in a missionary sales mode; meaning we had to convert the prospect with zero military exposure into believing in the value of military candidates. When these people would interview our military candidates, they were typically blown away by how talented they were. Frankly, most of our candidates were far superior to those they were used to interviewing. This was especially underscored when it came to our Enlisted candidates, who came from the technical world and were electricians, machinists, technicians and mechanics. Companies that would interview our candidates often gave them tests to assess their technical knowledge and aptitude. The pass rate for our candidates was frequently 10 times what it would be for their local candidates. The candidates they had previously been interviewing typically had a one in 20 pass rate, whereas our average was 10 in 20 and often surpassed that level.

We tried to connect with people in companies who had military experience, or at least were familiar with the military. When I was at TLG, we did a mailer to service academy graduates, who looked like they were in leadership positions in companies and might be interested in hiring other service academy graduates. Our hook line was "Harvard and Yale grads have been doing this for years. Isn't it time we did the same?" We sent out 554 mailers and received 67 replies, which was an astounding rate of return and enabled us to land more than 20 long-term hiring companies. This was truly a game changer, which primed the pump for the follow-on success we enjoyed.

There could be issues with inexperienced corporate recruiters. Typically, they were not first-generation college graduates, and had grown up in an area where there was not much exposure to the military. If there was, it was seldom with people who had enlisted. They were almost never anti-military, but were often military-ignorant. They just didn't understand that world.

What also contributed to this problem was once people shed their uniform, they typically moved on in their career, and if they wanted to be successful, did not become "military guy" within their company. They absorbed their new culture and, while not hiding that they had served, did not parade it around to make sure their fellow employees knew they had been in the military. As a result, many companies, even to this day, really don't know just how many veterans they have within their own ranks.

We constantly harped on going higher in companies, because the more senior and experienced people in the company often had some exposure in their career with seeing military people do well. It was a lot easier to let gravity work for us, by having senior people direct junior people to check out our operation, than it was for us to convince junior HR people to make our case for us. However, the issue was it took a lot of confidence for our ARs to contact senior people in a major company. Some were reluctant to do this, which is one of the reasons I made every new AR role play with me, as the final check to finish their initial training. I wanted them to gain the confidence that if they were able to get through me, they could handle talking to the senior people in Corporate America. I made my role play especially hard for that reason.

Most recruiting firms fill positions that have job specific requirements of A, B, C, and D skill sets or qualifications. Coming from the military, our candidates might have one of those listed requirements, maybe two, but never all four. Although our candidates didn't meet all of the specific requirements, once clients became aware of what skills the military candidates did have, they became very open to hiring our candidates. They realized military candidates provided leadership experience and technical aptitude, along with other positive attributes, which were far more important than the specific skill sets noted in the job requirements. The clients also realized that while our candidates would require some training, so would almost any civilian they would hire. They also knew our candidates were a blank slate when it came to corporate culture, and there would not be any bad habits to clean up that had been formed in another company.

Civilian Candidates versus Military Candidates

When I was at TLG, I had the opportunity to see what happened when military and civilian candidates competed head-to-head. Art Lucas had me take over the engineering (non-military) recruiting group, as they were having some issues and our military group was off to the races. Because some of the positions the civilian engineers interviewed for were identical to the ones my candidates were pursuing, it made some sense to try and make this a group effort. I had the bright idea of having the civilian candidates come to our HC. They could interview with a number of companies in one day, making the process much more efficient for them than it normally would have been. (No civilian HC equivalent existed to provide multiple interviews with different companies in the same day.) They were strong candidates, with true civilian engineering experience, from good schools like Clemson, Auburn and Georgia Tech. I really thought this would work out great.

I could not have been more wrong. Without exception, the military candidates crushed the civilian engineering candidates attending the same HC and interviewing for the same positions. I couldn't believe it! After trying this twice, I learned the military candidates, from a leadership perspective, talked about what they had done, while the civilian candidates talked about what they would do. Therein was the difference.

I learned there were three things strong technical leadership candidates had to have. These were hands-on technical experience, a strong academic background, and leadership experience. Civilian candidates had the first two, but what separated the military candidates was they had the leadership experience.

Why Do Companies Hire Military?

Some companies had so much success hiring military, it was in their DNA and was a priority in their annual recruiting plans. Other reasons included creating bench strength, affecting a cultural change of can-do in the ranks, and increasing diversity. One thing was a constant. Once they hired one military candidate, they always wanted more. Clients also liked our HC format. In a single day, they could interview 8-12 qualified candidates who had been screened and briefed on both the opportunity and the company. The client could then focus exclusively on identifying the fit, interviewing the candidates, getting to know them, and selling them on the opportunity without having to explain the details of the position. Doing this in the comfort of a first class hotel suite, in a desirable location, didn't hurt either.

Competitive Advantage

It was crucial our people knew what our competitive advantages were. They needed to understand why our military candidates were better than their civilian counterparts, and why we, as a firm, were better than our competition. They needed to really understand why a company would buy our product. Then, if they wanted to buy our product, why they would buy it from us. We knew why. A military candidate brings a lot to the table: drug-free, technical and leadership experience, consistently showing up for work every day, the ability to work as part of a team, documented performance history, geographic flexibility, experience in working with people of diverse cultures and backgrounds, language skills and thorough background checks. The U.S. government would also typically pay for the last move from wherever the candidates were stationed to wherever they were moving. With almost 100 HCs in locations from coast-to-coast, we had the capability to fill our clients' various positions nationally. BMI had a proven track record in placing diversity candidates. I also had the experience of running the TLG military operation nationally. While there are many things you only learn once you start a business, one thing I did NOT have to learn was how to generate placements. We were good, and our people needed to understand why.

Leads

Our ARs used the standard techniques on researching the companies they were targeting, and we had all of the necessary tools to help them. Some of our people were more creative than others, but a lot of their success stemmed from how hard they worked and how talented a salesperson they were. They were selling a blue-chip product, but nonetheless it took skill and persistence. However, to add to their sales kit, we augmented their efforts with a strong web presence, mailers, paying Google for keyword advertising and other areas of support. I called potential client mail-ins or call-ins layups and we eventually reached our goal of getting 100 per month, with one person dedicated to supporting this program.

The CRs were also crucial to this effort. They were on the frontlines, and knew which clients were hiring, and fed that information to our ARs so they could pursue those same companies. When you are in a sales business, it is crucial that your people feel like there is corporate support to help them. Many of our people knew the difference between them being successful, or wildly successful, was the corporate support they received. In addition, as companies attending our HCs were the life blood of our business, I wanted the ability to affect their attendance, and not be solely dependent on the varying talents of my people to do it themselves. Hence, what helped my ARs individually, benefited the entire company.

First Media

We had our first real experience with the media in a very unexpected way, and it only took us eight years to get it. We went to a Society for Human Resources Management trade show at the Atlanta World Congress Center, hoping to meet human resources people and get some business. We set up our table with some Army helmets on it, trying to garner some attention. It didn't really work out the way we had hoped, as many people initially thought we were helmet manufacturers.

However, a reporter from the Atlanta Journal-Constitution walked by our booth and asked us what we did. As the daughter of a retired Army Green Beret, she had grown up on military bases around the world. One thing led to another, and she interviewed both Sandy and me, then came to our office to take pictures. We ended up having a full-page spread on front page of the Atlanta Journal-Constitution Sunday Business Section. While our initial goal of meeting human resources executives and turning those meetings into business was unsuccessful, we ended up getting more publicity and exposure than we could have ever dreamed. That article was a significant part of our nomination packet, which helped us to be named Georgia Small Business Administration (SBA) Small Business of the Year two years later.

I ended up being the person who did most of the interviews and they were typically for newspapers or magazines. I was always a little wary about doing them, as your words could pretty much be sliced and diced whatever way the author wrote the article. However, ours were uniformly positive, both for us and for what we did.

Television

Bill Scott arranged for me to be interviewed on a one-hour program, Georgia Business, on Georgia Public Television. This nine-minute interview was a great opportunity, as the program was heavily watched and aired throughout the state. I was pretty nervous about it, because there would be no second chance and I didn't want to let my people down. Doing well would help them and doing poorly could embarrass both the company and them. In advance, I really prepped. Bill gave me extensive media interview training, and I did three subsequent practice interview sessions, each one increasing in level of difficulty. I did well enough in the practice sessions to at least feel like I could do OK.

In the studio waiting room, with makeup being applied, I sat next to a local basketball god, who was also being interviewed. He was going on before me, and was really relaxed and cool, in a way I certainly wasn't, as he had done this type of thing many times before. After he finished his interview, they called me out to the interviewer's table. I sat down and the red camera light went on. Showtime! The interviewer was great, and asked me many of the questions I came prepared to answer. We talked about the SBA award, and how Kennesaw State University helped us when we were trying to figure out how to organize our company. He then asked me why we didn't take out any loans when we started our company. I told him it never even dawned on us that anybody would consider loaning "us" any money. That got a big laugh. Afterwards, Bill thought I had done well and Sandy called me and said I did great. I was relieved.

Names Count

I found what you name something to be really important. I previously discussed PowerHire versus Mini-Conference, but there were others. There is a period of time when military candidates have transitioned out of the service, but are still trading on their military experience well after leaving the service. This is a period where they are still figuring out what they want to do, where they want to live, etc. We called these candidates Industry Experienced Candidates. We had a competitor call them Retreads. We called our Enlisted Technical candidates Enlisted Candidates. One competitor called them Miltechs – short for military technician. Our names communicated respect and the regard in which we held these candidates. Both areas were major placement areas for us. Using slang terms to describe something or someone is dangerous.

Testimonials

These were important. There were few things more powerful than candidates or clients saying we did a great job. We wanted to obtain testimonials we could publish on our website. We gathered these via a survey sent to clients post-HC. We asked four basic, yes or no questions, followed by space to fill out a testimonial, if they felt we had earned one. They could also recommend we talk to others in their company. In that way, we were able to get additional leads to further penetrate that company. We also sent surveys to our candidates. The number of testimonials we received numbered in the hundreds. Because they had checked the satisfied block on the survey, we could then declare, as part of our marketing, that 94 percent of our clients were satisfied with our services. I am convinced this survey worked so well because we told them in advance it would take less than a minute to fill out, which it did. We posted all of the testimonials on our website, as I wanted their sheer volume to be overwhelming and impressive to anybody who saw them.

Companies Recruiting Military on Their Own

There were some companies that made the decision to hire military, but to save paying military recruiting firm fees, decided to take it in-house and try doing it themselves. Most were unsuccessful and soon realized it was not so easy. The ones who were successful did some fundamental things right. They made a commitment in money, talent and time. They kept their military recruiters in place once they knew what they were doing. They created a culture within their company that understood and valued the military experience. In some respects, they created their own military recruiting firm, albeit with themselves as the only client. But most did not make a strong enough commitment, so typically, after a year or two, they were back to using us or one of our competitors once again.

CHAPTER 13

Compensation

Compensation plans need to be clear and easily understood. My future brother-in-law, who worked for IBM, thought TLG was taking advantage of my future wife, because she was unable to explain draw versus commission when she entered the recruiting world. It didn't help that prior to this, she had spent her career as a registered nurse with no experience in a sales environment. The sliding scale of commissions, which was pretty standard in a recruiting firm, contributed to the confusion. This was not limited to my wife. I made senior partner (commission level, not ownership) faster than anybody in the history of TLG, and I didn't even know there was a 10 percent bonus for all collections above $200K (which turned out to be a tidy sum of money for me). I also was a victim of not understanding things, when I was promoted to operations manager. I turned down a small base salary in exchange for the chance to make much more if our group made 10 percent increments over 100 percent of goal. What I didn't realize was being 120 percent of goal at the end of the quarter, didn't mean it would stay that way, since the goal was audited based on falloffs and costs incurred once the quarter was completed. Coming from the military, I didn't understand how all of this worked.

We simplified our commission rates at BMI. There was no sliding scale based on the revenue a recruiter brought in that quarter, only to revert to the lowest commission level at the beginning of the next quarter. Many companies think doing this motivates people to get to the next level, so they can make higher commissions. I just thought it was confusing.

We paid our senior managers based on a sales override versus a percentage of profits. There were too many areas they didn't have much ability to affect such as rent, payroll, equipment, legal, and travel (among other things), for them to be paid based on profits and not be distracted by things they couldn't control anyhow. Their focus needed to be on making as many placements as they could. While there was sometimes a lack of acknowledgement on their part about the need to not spend money, Sandy was foreboding enough to minimize most questions or complaints. The joke within BMI was to ask me if they wanted to spend money and ask Sandy if they wanted a day off.

One of the most important things I learned from Art Lucas was he never changed commission rates for people who were at a certain level or in a certain position. He might change the compensation for the next level or for the next person in that same position, but he never reduced it for one's current level. In a commission sales environment, there was tremendous security in knowing once you were at a certain level, it would not change. We modeled this.

The downside to this philosophy was that two people with the identical jobs could be paid at two different commission rates, based solely on who had started employment with the company earlier. I felt this was fair. There was security for each person, who knew their individual commission rate would be secured. Besides, if the person who began employment first had not done their job well, there might not even be a company to employ the person who started later.

Benefits

When we started, we didn't provide benefits, but we felt we should do something, so we gave each person $100 per month to help cover whatever policy they had. As we got our legs, we offered a 401k, along with comprehensive medical and dental coverage, and paid a sizable percentage of the premium. Sandy always did a remarkable job in keeping those premiums as low as possible.

Base salary versus commission

It might have been cheaper over the long run for us to provide a base salary when people started, eventually moving towards commission only, but that wasn't my mindset. I think I was a bit stubborn in this area, as I liked that all of my people had come up the hard way, like I did. My respect for them was enormous, as they had walked in my shoes.

Shaun G. Bradley

CHAPTER 14

Integrity Stories

Despite the commonly held perception that there are no ethics in business, I have seen firsthand people sacrificing some personal benefit or doing things they didn't have to do. You already read about Sandy insisting her previous company business be thrown into the BMI pot for both of us to share, even though she didn't have to do it. Here are couple more stories of personal sacrifice.

My friend, Eric Stagliano, is one of the founding fathers of the modern military recruiting industry. He created the template at TLG that countless others have used to sell the concept of hiring veterans to Corporate America. While placing military candidates had been done before, it had been on an ad hoc basis by small firms. Eric's techniques were easy to understand and easy to implement. Thousands of candidates, in many ways, owe their present positions to him, even if they don't know it.

However, before he entered the military recruiting world, he was working in another area of TLG, struggling and in backdraw just like I was. One day, a military candidate who he knew called into TLG. By rights, he was mine. Still, Eric already had the relationship with him and they were friends. The rules on this type of situation were somewhat vague, and we both ended up getting involved. As time progressed, we could see we were going to place him. I certainly didn't feel very good about this situation, and as I found out, neither did Eric. I finally went to Eric's manager to say that Eric should be given the billing for the placement,since the candidate should have been Eric's all along. Unknown to me, Eric had gone to my boss to say the candidate should be all mine, as he was a military candidate. It's easy to be magnanimous when things are rolling, but not so easy when you have nothing. We ended up splitting the placement, but a bond was formed between us, which lasts to this day.

Mary Butler, USNA '86, was managing the GE relationship for CDC as part of the massive GE hiring initiative, where the four firms were all working together. One of the rules for all of us was if any of the firms presented a candidate to GE, regardless of which division, then that firm would get the placement credit. This made sense, as GE was moving candidates internally from one division to another after the initial interview, depending on the fit and the candidate's preferences. We had previously set up an interview for a candidate with one particular GE division. There was no offer, and no additional movement was forthcoming.

One day I got a call from Mary, and she explained this same candidate accepted a GE offer earlier that day. Only then did he mention to her that he interviewed with another GE division through us. He added that it had gone nowhere and he appreciated her efforts in getting him into GE. Mary, knowing the rules, called me to say she didn't know he had interviewed with GE through us, that she was sorry, and would forward the check to us when it came in. I was flabbergasted that she even called to tell me, because there was no way we would have ever known.

I told her that while I appreciated both the call and her honesty, we didn't do anything to deserve the placement and shouldn't receive any money. She insisted we take the money, and I equally insisted that we not. To this day, it might be one of the most unusual conversations I've ever had. Finally, after continuing to argue about this, she said that when the check came in, she was just going to mail it to me. I told her she was free to do that, but we wouldn't cash it. Finally she said, "OK, if you really feel that way." She left the business a few years later to be a stay-at-home mom, but she remains a giant in my eyes.

CHAPTER 15

SBA Award

There are a lot of awards given to businesses; the county, the city, the local newspapers, and other entities all give them. There is only one given by the U.S. government for small businesses. How we were even nominated for this award makes for an interesting story.

Sandy and I had been wrestling with how to organize our company as we grew. We had offices in multiple locations, yet distinct business Disciplines focused on specific areas. Was it better to organize by location or by Discipline? This was a really important decision, and we weren't sure what direction to take.

Each had its advantages. If we organized by location, there would probably be more cohesion at the local level, with somebody in charge of the entire location, but possibly at the expense of in-depth expertise within each area. If we organized by Discipline, we might have better control and expertise at the national level (similar to a brand manager), but we might be sacrificing something at the local level.

We were really unsure what to do. I remember telling Sandy that we couldn't be the first company to have had this issue. I thought maybe the local university, Kennesaw State, might be able to help us. I called and told them what we were looking for, and they said they had people on staff who were consultants and handled things just like this for local businesses. I asked how much it cost. They said, "It's free. It's funded by the state to help people just like you."

It sounded too good to be true, but we made an appointment and met with three PhD's from the Michael J. Coles College of Business. They were awesome. They asked us the questions that helped us to answer our own questions. When we left, Carlotta Roberts, who was running the program, said wanted to nominate us for the United States SBA Small Business of the Year Award, as they thought we had a really good story to tell and would be very competitive. I remember telling Sandy afterwards that I guess they didn't think we were too screwed up, if they wanted to nominate us for an award. We walked in telling them about all of our issues and problems, asking for help finding solutions. We walked out nominated for an award. This set things in motion for us to eventually win this very prestigious honor. And by the way, we organized by Discipline, with the Discipline heads setting policy and providing expertise, but with local command and control of actual operations, so we split the difference.

In May, 2001, we were honored locally at the 2001 SBA Award Luncheon at the Cobb Galleria. All of our people attended and were seated at the front table to share in this honor, as they had made it possible. In a proud moment for me, my dad flew down from Green Bay to be there as well. Then it was on to Washington, DC, to accept the national award.

This event was really extraordinary. While we had to pay our own way to get there, it was not something we were going to miss. Libby and I went up a day early and did some touring. We went to The National Archives, the U.S. Mint, and the Smithsonian Museums. That night we also took a carriage ride through the capitol. The night was chilly, but we saw everything on a memorable three-hour ride.

The following day we registered and received all of our knickknacks and brochures. The first night, Microsoft was the sponsor, so the food and drinks were big-time. We received our award (Sandy and I each received one), which was a miniature marble Washington Monument. We stood in line to receive our awards and it reminded me of the Miss America pageant, with each state winner being introduced in alphabetical order. We went right after Florida.

The next day, we had a luncheon hosted by the U.S. Department of Commerce. It was very nice and I'll never forget the speech given by Secretary of Commerce Donald Evans. He was introduced by the head of the U.S. Small Business Administration, who spoke of how the Secretary had grown a Texas oil tooling company to great heights under his leadership. (The Secretary was a friend of President George W. Bush from Midland, Texas.) However, the Secretary didn't talk about the good times. Instead, he spoke about the responsibility he felt towards his people to keep them employed when oil prices crashed. It was refreshing to hear someone at his level talk about the things we all felt.

The next day we went to the White House. Even though I graduated from the Naval Academy, served on active duty, and had been in the Pentagon, I had never gone to the White House. We were directed to the East Room, which is where the formal recognition ceremonies are held.

While there were 53 winners (50 states and the three territories), the overall winner left an unforgettable impression on me. He was an African-American man from Alabama, who had started his construction company in 1972. His nickname was Honest John. His face looked like it was made out of granite. This was one impressive man. I could only imagine and respect how hard it must have been for him to earn this award.

While in the East Room, I happened to be sitting next to the winner from Iowa, who was a graduate of my high school archrival, Green Bay East. We talked to each other about how much we missed legendary Kroll's hamburgers (a restaurant located across from Lambeau Field). The winner from Wisconsin was the owner of Culver's (a major Midwest fast food chain), who was seated one row directly in front of us. He overheard our conversation and turned around to tell us about Culver's, and how their hamburgers were better than Kroll's. It struck me how far we had all come to be sitting in the White House, yet talking about where the best hamburgers in Green Bay were made.

Libby volunteered to try to get pictures of Sandy and me with President Bush. However, after the ceremony, he quickly left via a side entrance, which happened to be where Libby had set up to take our pictures. She was alone and he stopped, shook her hand, and said, "Thank you so much for coming." Very nice.

As we left the White House, it reminded me of my time at USNA, when I sometimes thought, "How in the hell did I ever get here?" and

"Did I really deserve to be?" We were the babies, being among the youngest people there and having a company with the fewest number of years in existence. I was amazed by the lack of arrogance among the winners. I think we all knew a fundamental truth – had a bullet landed a little bit to the left or a little bit to the right, we would not only not be at the White House receiving an award, but we probably wouldn't even still be in business.

It was almost as if we had been given this award before we had earned it. Despite how hard it was to start our company, we were now going to have to really earn it, because as the plane took off and we returned to Atlanta, the recession of 2001-2004 was hitting. We were now going to have to show we were worthy of this award.

CHAPTER 16

Recruiting Military Candidates

As we were recruiting the military equivalent of the four and five star players the big-time football programs were going after, finding them was not hard. Convincing them to use us as their recruiting firm was the key. We had competitors who required candidates to work exclusively with them as their sole military recruiting firm. We were OK with our candidates using other firms or other sources. We felt confident in our ability to place them and, besides, we didn't have the information on every position in Corporate America anyhow.

Diversity Recruiting

As the first major U.S. institution to desegregate, the military has always been a place of upward mobility for minorities. Although certainly not without its issues, on balance, minorities have fared better in the military than in many other places. Most Historically Black Colleges and Universities (HBCUs) have strong ROTC programs, and many urban high schools have great ROTC programs as well. When I began my career in recruiting, the business world had made the hiring of qualified minority candidates a major priority. It is debatable whether this was for Affirmative Action reasons, to remedy a white, male-only hierarchy in their company, to avoid a public relations problem, or to simply look for the best talent in every place they could. The bottom line was diversity recruiting was important to them.

When we started BMI, I knew having talented minority candidates would be a competitive advantage. So, before we even opened our doors, I spent three days at the Naval Academy buried in the stacks of Nimitz

Library going through the West Point, Air Force Academy and Naval Academy yearbooks, writing down the names of every minority graduate, both male and female, going back to 1960. I knew who they were, which in recruiting is half the battle.

While many of the big companies wanted to use us to hire talented minority candidates, many of them didn't understand the military all that well. They were interested in hiring minority candidates who were veterans as a means of recruiting talented minorities - not necessarily to hire veterans. However, seeing the sheer talent level of military candidates, opened their eyes, and the hiring of veterans became an area of focus for them. It has always struck me as interesting that minority veterans being recruited by Corporate America provided the pathway for many non-minority veterans to also be given their opportunity.

On the subject of diversity, one of the truly underappreciated parts of the military experience is the exposure to other people in the military who do not look or think like you, or have a background different from yours. No matter the background, people in military units must learn to work together as a team. Add to this an exposure to cultures in other parts of the world, and you cannot help but be sensitized to the fact there are other ways to view things, and that your opinion might not be the only one worthwhile.

Female officers were also a focus for us. Almost without exception, they were outstanding. Many of the positions we filled were in manufacturing plants, warehouses, or in a facility other than an office building. It was particularly attractive to our clients that most of our female candidates had not only succeeded in a challenging and mechanized environment, but had also worked in a male-dominated world. Also, the fact they had technical degrees or technical experience made them very much in demand.

Placing diversity candidates was a priority from the day we opened our doors through my last day, with 29 percent of all of our placements being minority or female candidates. This is a stat that still makes me proud.

Candidates Stationed Overseas

Candidates stationed overseas had unique problems in transitioning from the military. We travelled overseas to meet them, and even had CRs living there to establish relationships with them. However, even with us doing those things, it was just harder for those candidates. They really had two choices. They could come home to attend an HC and stick around for a few weeks, hoping their second interviews could all take place within that time frame, so they could receive and accept an offer. They would then know where they were going to live and work when they came back permanently. Their other option was to return to the states, leave the service and then start their career search. Neither alternative was as good as what the candidates stationed stateside had, but we worked with them as best we could. Some companies would travel overseas to get a jump on the great talent available, but not many made that effort. Most focused on filling their own needs as soon as possible, and avoided the uncertainty of waiting for an overseas candidate to return.

Key Candidates

To target the candidates we needed, we established a Key Candidate Program for our Officer candidates. These were the candidates whose profile comprised 90 percent of our Officer placements. A candidate could not be considered Key unless that candidate had at least one of the targeted credentials. We created a point system where each sought after credential received one point. Points were given to service academy graduates, diversity candidates, and Navy Nukes, in addition to candidates having maintenance/logistics experience or having a hard science (physics, chemistry) or engineering degree.

For example, any service academy graduate who had a B.S. in Electrical Engineering would get two points, one for being an academy graduate and one for being a degreed engineer. Some candidates had three or four points. This system served to focus our recruiting efforts, as the CRs were measured on how many points their candidates had and how many of their Key candidates were at an HC. The CRs were allowed to bring in non-Key candidates, but there were always more of them than we needed. This forced the CRs to only bring in outstanding non-Key candidates.

This was a great program. Everyone in the company wanted to know how many Key candidates were coming to the HC. The ARs didn't always understand everything about an HC, but they certainly understood that having a lot of Key candidates meant they would be in good shape, if they brought their clients to an HC that had a lot of Key candidates coming to it.

Another important advantage to this system was being able to forecast how many Key candidates we had in the pipeline. We could then make adjustments to remedy those areas where we did not have good numbers, well in advance of when we needed them.

We had our best CRs recruit the high-profile areas. This meant diversity technical candidates, as well as Navy Nuke Officers. These were the must-have areas. Having numbers in these categories ensured we would get the big-name clients to attend our HC. And, if we had these candidates, then typically our competition did not.

Enlisted Recruiting

In many ways, placing Enlisted candidates was a more efficient and cleaner operation than recruiting Officers. We focused so clearly on recruiting candidates from the technical fields that we didn't have the issue of trying to place a candidate who didn't have the profile we needed. Also, terms of enlistment are clearly spelled out, so there was a much more defined timeline for recruiting them, as opposed to that of Officers who had a lot more flexibility on when they could leave the service once they completed their initial commitment.

As there were so many more Enlisted candidates than Officers, it required a significant infrastructure to recruit and manage their numbers. Our size enabled us to do this, with most of our competition without this capability. This was why most firms that recruit military people only place Officers. From a business perspective, there were a lot more Enlisted candidates, and a lot fewer people recruiting them, which was a beautiful thing. Our focus by Discipline also made a difference. Our Enlisted operation was never treated as an adjunct extension of the Officer Discipline, as it could easily have become, had we not separated these areas. We ended up placing triple the number of Enlisted candidates as Officers and this was a big reason.

One of the biggest differences in recruiting Enlisted people was the relationships with the candidates tended to be six months or less in duration, whereas our relationships with the Officer candidates were often much longer. Typically, Enlisted candidates did not enter a career search mode until they were much closer to their separation date, compared to what was standard for most Officer candidates. We did the same things for our Enlisted candidates that we did for our Officers (resume help, career guidance, interview prep, and completed file), but in a much more condensed time frame.

Industry Experienced Candidates

Until candidates have established a solid civilian career, where their civilian experience is now going to be what helps them get their next job, they naturally will continue to use their military experience to market themselves. This time frame can often last up to five years from the date they left active duty. While military candidates have a long list of great qualities, just like new college graduates, they are often still unsure of what they want to do or where they want to live. We found industry experienced candidates to be even better than they were when they initially left the service. They tended to be more focused on what they wanted, and had more realistic expectations after experiencing the civilian world. However, there was never a steady flow or enough of them to meet the candidate demand our HCs required. While they often did participate in our HCs, the primary vehicle for placing them was via OC interviews.

Geographically Restricted Candidates

Typically, candidates who were geographically restricted were tied to metro areas. There were certain metro areas, such as Atlanta, Chicago,

Dallas and Los Angeles, where we could help them. However, it was important to manage the expectations of these candidates, and not have them think they were going to be able to count on us to find them a job. Placing them in a specific, limited location could only be done on an exception basis. It was also important the CRs not spend the same amount of time with these candidates, who were a lot less likely to be placed, than with candidates who were open to more locations. Being upfront about what we would be able to do or not do for the candidates was the key.

Selecting Versus Recruiting

I always felt unbelievable anxiety when I was a frontline recruiter to have enough quality candidates to support the ARs job orders. I always wanted more. Enough was never enough. Because I had good numbers, I was able to fight the natural urge to see qualities in candidates I needed, rather than the qualities they actually had. Desperation causes you to lower your standards. Even when I no longer recruited, I never lost that need for us to have more candidates than we needed. However, there was always a feeling of trying to balance your need for a candidate with control of that candidate. You worried if you pushed too hard, you might push the candidate away. However, the reality was the stronger you were, and the more confident you were, the better the candidates responded, because they wanted somebody to control the process, in a world where they didn't know or understand very much.

I remember an HC where I was loaded with Navy Nukes, which was unusual because they were in so much demand and you never had enough. I had a Navy Nuke candidate who was serving as a Navy ROTC instructor at North Carolina State, while getting his M.S. in Mechanical Engineering, along with already having an undergraduate engineering degree. Obviously, he had credentials, but he was arrogant, and I didn't really like him. He was pushing me about why he should even use us when he had access to the career placement services at North Carolina State. Why should he travel all the way to Atlanta to attend an HC? The capabilities of most college placement offices pale in comparison to what a national military recruiting firm like ours could offer, but he didn't believe that (or so I thought). Finally, I just got tired of dealing with him and told him, "Look, I don't think we're right for you, and you probably shouldn't come to our HC. You come across as arrogant, so why don't you just use the placement office." The next day he called me and said, "I'm sorry Mr. Bradley. I was a jerk. I am really sorry. Can I please come to your Hiring Conference?" I did let him attend the HC. He showed up with a good attitude, and we successfully placed him. This underscored to me the lesson of being in control of the candidate relationship.

The Hunt

I always loved "The Hunt." Finding candidates and then getting them to work with me was always exhilarating. I felt if I could touch them, I could get them, and if I could get them, my competitors would then be chasing me. Our candidates were really outstanding. For people that good to place their future employment in my hands was a responsibility I never took for granted. These people had choices and they chose me – what a great feeling! We were relentless in searching for candidates, finding them any way and any place we could – many times in unexpected places.

I remember seeing a West Point bumper sticker on a car in an Atlanta grocery store parking lot, so I put my business card inside the windshield wiper. It was the car of the mother of two West Pointers. I would eventually place both of them. I also found Jim O'Neal, who is currently the long-time manager of TLG Atlanta Office and a great friend of mine, by calling every Jim O'Neal in the Atlanta telephone book (there were more than 20). I met him a few years earlier, but had lost touch. I knew he was from Atlanta, and hoped to find either him or his dad, if Jim was a junior. His sister took the message, and Jim found his way to me.

Interviewing Questions

Identifying strong candidates early, and then building relationships with them, was crucial. Meeting with them, advising them, and answering their questions were all part of it. When I interviewed candidates, I never asked the standard interview questions like, "Tell me about yourself" or

"What is your biggest weakness?" Instead, I always found something either on their resume or in their background that interested me. You can't fake interest. I was learning something from them, and the candidates could sense I was interested in them. I could always, later on, learn what I needed to know about their particular situation, but the most important thing was making that connection.

My Own Territory

I recruited a candidate territory for the first five years we were in business. By working a territory, I was able to lead by example, which was probably the best training I ever did. Instead of telling my people how to do it, they were able to observe me actually recruit. This also enabled me to distribute some of my own territory to the other CRs once they proved themselves. As we grew, it was a lot easier to give away some of my own territory, than it was to take some away from another CR.

Targeting Academy Grads

We made an effort to touch EVERY service academy graduate who was in the window to either leave or begin to think about leaving the service (3-8 years after graduation). This changed every year, as a new year group was moving into the recruiting window. About 1,000 individuals graduate every year from the three major academies, and another 250 graduate from the Coast Guard Academy. Some of my people thought doing this was unattainable, but I knew, even if we didn't get them all, trying to get as many as we could, would yield a major competitive advantage. Getting the names was not difficult as they are published annually in the Army, Navy and Air Force Times and certainly pre-9/11 you could get this info (along with their unit assignments) by submitting Freedom of Information Act requests. We also subscribed to the various base newspapers, many of which were free. The monthly alumni magazines from the academies also provided info. This was a huge undertaking, but the results of our efforts were impressive, as we had so many Academy graduates responding to our mailers that our CRs almost couldn't process them all.

Common Gates

Unlike traditional search recruiting, there were common gates most of our candidates passed through. For us, knowing where these gates were made it easier to both find them and touch them. We had the ability to touch virtually every person in the military with our billet mailers. We knew the name, organizational structure, and mailing address of almost every military unit or organization. We could then target specific billets, knowing the person currently filling the position would have a high likelihood of possessing the type of background and experience we were looking to recruit. Our billet mailing system evolved over time, as the units and mailing addresses, along with the types of people we were looking for, changed.

For example, establishing Disciplines in IT/Telecom and Medical necessitated an entirely new set of units and billets to be targeted. In the early years, we stuffed our own envelopes, and I insisted on signing each one in blue ink, so each candidate would know I had personally signed every one. Eventually, the sheer volume of mailers we were sending (250,000 annually at our peak) ended this practice, and we brought our direct mail capability in-house by leasing the equipment and hiring a retired Navy Chief Petty Officer with recruiting experience to manage this crucial area.

We also learned about, and sometimes joined, professional organizations, which enabled us to touch the targeted candidates. One such organization was the National Naval Officer Association, which is an organization of minority Navy, Marine and Coast Guard Officers. I joined this organization, and was even able to be a guest speaker at one of their chapter meetings.

Base Trip Presentations

Our CRs made frequent trips to the various military bases in their assigned territories, as meeting the candidates in person was a crucial part of our entire process. We were able to sell the candidates on our services, as well as evaluate them to see if they were a fit for us and our clients.

I felt the best way was to individually call the candidates we wanted to talk with, and schedule one-on-one interviews with each of them. Our support staff also sent the CRs bio to the candidates well ahead of time. By making the entire invitation more structured and formal, the candidates took it seriously and few missed their initial appointments. This was sometimes rough on our CRs, who had to make the same presentation over and over to a new candidate throughout the day, but it ensured we got our shot at touching them. The alternative method, and the way most of our competitors did it, was to rent a ballroom, market the event and see who showed up. I hated the lack of control this presented, so we did it differently.

SACC Disaster

The service academies conduct a job fair called the Service Academies Career Conference (SACC), which is exclusively for academy graduates who are in transition or thinking about leaving the service. Four are conducted annually at various locations around the country. I was an occasional guest on a panel held the night before the job fair began, which provided interview prep for the attendees, along with an overview on how the job fair worked. This was a condensed version of what we provided to our candidates at the HC. After the presentation, there was a Q & A session that did not go well for me. I was challenged about our company advising service academy graduates who were liberal arts majors to also list on their resume that they had a General Engineering degree.

We made that recommendation because few people are aware that even English majors at the Naval Academy will take three semesters of calculus, a year of physics, a year of chemistry, a year of electrical engineering, thermodynamics, stability of solids, meteorology, computer science, and weapons system rocketry, along with a host of other technical courses. In four years, a graduate will complete 144-146 academic credit hours, none of which are for physical education. The other service academies are similar. A recruiter or human resources manager, who graduated from a civilian school, will automatically assume any English major would never take any of these technical courses, or even have that many credit hours.

As many of our job openings required a technical degree, the unfortunate result was too often, very qualified Academy graduates wouldn't even be given the chance to interview, because their resumes did not reflect the true scope of their collegiate coursework. When we tried to explain a service academy curriculum to the interviewers in an attempt to remedy this situation, they just became more confused. Remember, many of them didn't understand the military very well to begin with. Listing General Engineering on the resume was an attempt to solve this issue.

The problem is there actually is a General Engineering degree at the Naval Academy. So, in front of a group of 150 service academy graduates who were in the panel audience, I was challenged on what we were advising candidates to do. I tried to explain why we recommended doing it this way, but it did not go well. I looked either like an idiot or, more likely, that I was trying to pull a fast one, which I was not. Anyhow, after that fun event, I gave it a lot of thought. We changed our advice, and subsequently recommended academy graduates without an engineering degree put "general engineering core curriculum" on their resume, in addition to their major, which was more accurate anyhow.

Working with Transition Offices

Transition Offices are organizations set up on military bases to help veterans transition to civilian life. One of their missions is to assist them in finding employment. Some of these outfits viewed us as helpful, as we were positioned to help many of the people in their program find civilian employment. Some, unfortunately, perceived us as a threat, thinking our existence might impact theirs. One of the challenges that plagued transition offices was their inability to document their results in helping veterans find employment. Frankly, they didn't have the staff to track down the veterans who had gone through their program and find out where they had gone to work, if at all. Conversely, the veterans had no incentive to call back to let them know and thank them for their assistance. Nonetheless, a program like this was a step forward for the services. They began to think they had some obligation to the service members as they left the military, and not just care about them only for what they could do while on active duty.

Candidate File

The candidate's file was an important part of the recruiting process. The information we required was pretty straightforward, and included a resume, college transcripts, military evaluations, references, and their application. It also provided a structure for many of our conversations. The responsiveness of the candidates in providing us with what we needed also told us how serious they were about their career search, as well as how strong they viewed their relationship with us. Having all of their paperwork in order also guaranteed they had what they needed for their interviews, along with ensuring we had it in the event a client asked for it.

Candidate Application

We required every candidate to complete an extensive application. This became THE source document, and was far more important for us than a standard application could ever be. Many resumes, but particularly those of military people who have never written a resume before, are lacking crucial information that could help them be attractive to a prospective employer. For the candidate's benefit, our application provided information on those details they might overlook that could help us sell their credentials to a client. It also helped us evaluate the candidate and ascertain landmines, which would help us decide whether to work with a candidate.

We also learned useful information, such as how they heard about BMI or what other companies had already interviewed them. We were also able to obtain information on their type of discharge, and whether they had a criminal record or significant traffic violations. This information was important, because if the issue was minor, and in the past, we could address it in advance with the client, so it would not be a roadblock if there was interest in the candidate. As all of this information was fed into RW, we evolved to the point where we could match Military Occupational Specialties (MOS) against our job orders, and not be solely dependent on how well the CRs remembered their candidates' skill sets. This was particularly important for our Enlisted candidates, who were being hired for positions requiring specific technical skills and aptitudes. This was a major undertaking, as knowing and explaining MOS' was a herculean task, because there are so many and they are so varied.

We also needed to know when the candidates could begin employment. Knowing their last date of active duty was crucial. Our clients had openings they wanted and needed to fill. Some candidates wanted to start work immediately and some wanted a couple of weeks break. We needed to know which it was.

Job Boards

I agreed to allow us to use the various electronic job boards as one more additional tool to find candidates, but I really hated doing it. Yes, we did get some candidates by using them. However, they were frequently those who were either not high quality or had already been through interviews with other firms or companies. In some respects, they were like road kill that had already been picked over. By the time we contacted them, we were already late to the party. I wanted us in there early, having already developed a great relationship with the candidates, well before they would even have a resume to post on a job board. When used best, they were one final check to find candidates we might have missed. However, my concern that they provided a crutch for my CRs never really went away.

Placement Announcements

Prospective candidates needed to be continually touched. One of the best ways was to send them announcements of successful placements, especially for candidates with a similar background to theirs. Many times the candidates would know the placed candidate personally. This also served to reassure candidates that we were going to be able to help them.

RIF's

The military often has layoffs, although that's never what they're called. They call it a "reduction in force." Sometimes entire year groups were decimated by large numbers of people being forced out of the service, or being given the opportunity to leave before they had completed their service commitment. When this happened, we learned to look past them not completing their service obligation, as many of them were great candidates, who were simply a victim of events beyond their control.

Competition

One of the things I lived for was when we wemt head-to-head against one of our competitors, and we both had an HC on the same day and in the same city, which made it impossible for the candidates to attend both. When we won those battles, it meant our competitor had lost. When my CRs won those recruiting contests, I made a big deal about it.

CHAPTER 17

Recruiting Our Own

What I Looked for in Potential Hires

I was often asked what qualities I looked for in a potential hire. I always wanted somebody who was more afraid of failure than somebody who wanted to succeed. Fear of failure comes from some insecurity, no doubt, where failure is so personally devastating to them they do everything they can to prevent it from happening. They never forget their failures. In fact, they remember them much more than they ever remember their successes.

I didn't want to hire "golden boys" whose life had been easy for them simply because they were so smart, talented and good-looking. I knew that no matter how much success they had already experienced, if they did what we did, they were going to fail, and fail often, and they better have some experience in getting up off of the mat and re-entering the arena. I really tried to learn where they had failed, and failed hard, and what they did about it. I wanted to hire people who had tasted real failure, and would do what it took to avoid having to experience that feeling again. And when they would fail, as they surely would in our business, were resilient enough to bounce back instead of being crushed by it. Sometimes this information was not easy to discover, because candidates try to avoid giving those types of answers, but I was typically able to learn it.

Staffing BMI

While the nature of our business was recruiting veterans, the most important recruiting was done in hiring our own people, and we never stopped looking. We found them everywhere. One of our stars was our waiter at a company luncheon. He had just graduated from a very good college, where he was captain of the baseball team. He had just moved to Atlanta, and was waiting on tables to pay the bills until he found something better. Another star was a referral from Sandy's chiropractor. One was even a service academy graduate, who was the son of a Career Warrant Officer I had served with in Spain.

Many of our people obviously came from the military, and a lot had been athletes, either in high school or college (both male and female). As a result, we sent letters to the athletic directors and coaches at small colleges, asking them to send us athletes who they thought might be a fit. Most of the time they were glad to send us people, as they tried to help their good kids. We stayed away from the big schools. Our eyes were opened when we attended a "jock career fair" at the University of Texas, which the athletes were required to attend. Many of the male athletes still had dreams of pro careers, and were attending only because it was mandatory. Most of them were unimpressive. The female athletes were entirely different. They were unbelievable – smart, articulate, fit, well dressed – the whole package. However, they were looking for big-time opportunities with big companies, and didn't understand how a small (in their eyes) company like ours would be attractive to them.

ARs Coming from the Military.

In the early days of our company, our successful ARs were women who were disproportionately not from the military. However, this changed over time, and we had many successful ARs who were both male and had prior military experience. Most were former officers, but not all. Our military ARs had the advantage of being able to talk the lingo and describe the product. They were the product!

Non-Military Account Representatives

Without question, our non-military ARs were true believers in our military candidates. They were able to translate the military background to hiring managers, who didn't have military experience. They learned the military vernacular, and knew what it was like to not initially understand it. Thus, they were able to place themselves in the shoes of the person who didn't understand, and explain it in a way they could grasp.

Targeted Military

We found success with military candidates, who held particular positions while serving. We sent a specific mailer to individuals in those billets, inviting them to interview with us. We targeted positions, which were filled by officers and senior enlisted people, who had been handpicked by their commanders to fill critical and visible positions that required polish and strong interpersonal skills. These positions included Army Battalion Adjutants (the Battalion Commander's right-hand person for administration), the General and Admiral Flag Aides, and those who were directly responsible for recruiting college students to become Commissioned Officers. This was easily among the best things we ever did, which yielded a long list of BMI heavy hitters.

Things That Didn't Work

We thought hiring people who had prior staffing industry experience or had worked in sales at a major company would be a home run. Almost without exception, they failed. We thought their experience would be a plus, but the reality was, if they were any good, they probably would have never left their current company or industry. Talent was a lot better indicator of success than experience, as I never forgot from my time with the young watch captains on the Mess Decks on my ship. As a result, we disregarded prior sales or civilian recruiting experience. We wanted people with a history of excellence, who we liked and whose personal baggage wouldn't torpedo them. We could train our people. We couldn't create talent or character.

Recruiting Candidate Recruiters

In many respects, it was easy to identify CRs and recruit them. Leadership ability, communication skills, personal impact, and a strong military record were all key elements in doing that job well. It also did not require the cold calling skills our ARs needed to develop. This position also appealed to those who had a desire to help people who were just like them when they left the service. It also attracted people who were looking for something that wasn't necessarily mainstream. I wanted my CRs to have a WOW factor and they did.

Stereotypes

I consider myself pretty open-minded, but sometimes you needed to check yourself. Our Norfolk office had been interviewing a rock band guitar player to be an AR. When I found out, I was wondering what my people could possibly have been thinking. Every image in my mind of him was of somebody with long, stringy hair, covered in tattoos, taking every illegal drug known to man. Apparently, he was a personal referral from somebody in the office. When I eventually met him, I was blown away, and could not have been more wrong. He was clean-cut, in shape, a gifted athlete, and a great guy, who just happened to like playing guitar in a rock band. He would go on to be a superstar at BMI. He also recruited one of his band mates to join us as well, who would also go on to become a superstar. I started telling my people that maybe we should only be recruiting ARs from rock bands. I was wrong. Boy, was I wrong. I learned a lesson about stereotyping.

Sandy and I Did the Interviewing

One of the things that always made a difference to our candidates was how senior the person was who did the interview. This sent a powerful message to our candidates, as to how important to the company they really were. Some companies, Home Depot, Otis Elevator and Daimler-Chrysler, among others, did this very well by scheduling special forums, where their senior people came in for the express purpose of interviewing military candidates. However, nobody did it better than H. Ross Perot. He gave an address to all of the candidates at the SACC, and almost verbatim said, "The reason I'm here is to recruit you. If you were as important to the rest of these companies as you are to me, the CEOs of those companies would be here to recruit you like I am." Powerful stuff and, of course, being a prominent Naval Academy graduate didn't hurt either. As you would expect, he cleaned up. This was not lost on us. Sandy or I personally interviewed almost everybody.

Most of the people we were interviewing were already interested in us. They saw the camaraderie and energy BMI had, and they sensed at some level that if this many great people were here, then there must be something pretty good and pretty special going on. We also made sure they saw the sales charts. These people were smart and could run the numbers quickly. They saw that besides having a lot of fun, our people were also making a lot of money. We knew we had a good thing and while making the pot of gold was a real possibility for them, we didn't sugarcoat that the startup was difficult and this was a tough business. We emphasized they would not be doing anything differently than what our other people had already done, and that Sandy and I also travelled the same road. The military candidates, in particular, ate this up.

From a recruiting perspective, having people who had been successful for years, and having potential new people meet them, enabled us to continue to bring on new people. Winners want to be with winners. I think it is crucial that your long-termers be happy campers. Recruits will look to see how long people have been with your company. If you don't have some who have been with you for a significant length of time (and your company is not a startup), the obvious question people will ask themselves is, "Why not?"

Competition with Our Clients for a Candidate

An area where we had to figure out our rules of the road was when we were in competition with one of our own clients for the same candidate. How could we be taking care of the client, when we were at the same time trying to get the same candidate to come to work for us? We also had the issue with our own people, who would not make the placement if the candidate ended up working at BMI. We decided the solution was to let everybody know upfront what was going on. We competed hard for a candidate we wanted, as did the client and our own people, but transparency was the key.

Shaun G. Bradley

CHAPTER 18

Development / Training

Training

We created an AR and CR training manual, and had formal training for our new people when they started, but that was only the beginning. Our people worked in close proximity to each other, and we had an environment where our senior people were truly helpful to new people. Our new people had the great advantage of learning by just picking up what was in the air every day. Too often, training consists of one class that is expected to make a person proficient. My observation is training, to be effective, needs to be of short duration and continually reinforced. Ours was.

As I previously mentioned, I required every new AR to complete a successful role play with me before they could begin calling on actual prospects. This became a rite of passage all of our sales people had to get through. One of my people (one of the rock band guys) called me to do his role play while I was on vacation. When my wife answered the phone, she told him how much I would love his aggressiveness, so I let him knock out his role play while we were at Hilton Head. This story got around, and soon enough I was getting calls on weekends and at night (obviously, we didn't call actual clients at night or on the weekend), which I also loved because it showed some degree of fearlessness. This eventually got out of control. My wife and I went to a movie and when we came home, our babysitter had taken down 10 messages from a couple of people repeatedly trying to get their role play done. I thought it was pretty funny, but our sitter did not. The next day I put the word out that role play calls on weekends and at night were now out of bounds.

CR Philosophy on Territories

I really tried to NOT have our CRs recruit from the area of the military where they had previously served. This may seem counterintuitive, but I wanted them to grow strong and confident, and having them learn a new area of the military forced that issue. I had very high standards in hiring CRs and thought they should be able to learn a new area, and it would limit their growth if they were able to lean on what they already knew. It was also what I had done, and I knew it was a better way. When I was a frontline CR, I often knew more about Army units and organizations than the Army candidates I was interviewing. When they asked me what unit I had been in, and I told them I was prior Navy, I knew I had them. They assumed if I knew as much about their service community as I obviously did, then I must know everything about recruiting. I wanted my CRs to be in that same position.

CR Training

As part of every CR's initial training, I reviewed the things I learned as a CR that had made a difference for me. This carried a lot of weight as I was viewed, both internally and externally, as one of the founding fathers of what the industry had become. Things I emphasized were technology, time, candidate control, and knowing your candidates. On technology, I stressed that I had never seen a placement occur without a handshake or a phone call. While email, texting and other forms of easy communication were great, they tended to help only after a relationship with the candidate had already been established. There was no way any sane person was going to take a position, without some trust having been previously built with the company and/or the recruiter.

I pointed out candidates valued their own time a lot more than the time of their recruiters. There was a tendency to do a lot of work for the candidates. I cautioned them that it was important to make the candidates invest time in working with us. Frequently, that involved having candidates drive to Atlanta or to our other locations to see us in our offices. While not always necessary to accomplish what was required, these candidates were more likely to come to our HC, instead of our competitor's, because they had invested time in us. I also put emphasis on how to deal with a cancelled appointment, whether it was in our offices or if we had travelled to a military base to conduct interviews.

Obviously, things came up, and the easy way and the natural tendency, especially as our CRs were prior military and understood what could happen, was to tell the candidates we understood, and would reschedule the appointment and get it next time. CRs would want to make sure the relationship was maintained. I told them they needed to make the cancellation of a scheduled appointment not so easy. Candidates needed to understand we took scheduled appointments seriously and considered them commitments. In the future, that little conversation would prevent them from cancelling on us again and, if it came to it, they would cancel on one of our competitors before they would cancel on us.

I also told my CRs, as long as they were always honest with the candidates, and the candidates knew they were hustling to help them get opportunities, they would forgive a misstep here or there. However, I warned them candidates would never forgive not knowing their story. They couldn't be reading a file to help them remember who the candidate was. They had to know as soon as they saw the candidate or heard their name. That was the standard.

Not Becoming Friends with Candidates

It was important our CRs, especially when they first started, not overly identify with the candidates they were recruiting. As our CRs had done many of the same things, or had been to the same places as the candidates we were trying to recruit, keeping a healthy professional distance was important and not always easy to do. Crossing this line resulted in candidates being poorly evaluated, and created confusion on the candidates' part on just what our relationship was to them. I told my CRs that they didn't go to a doctor or a dentist or an attorney looking for a friend, and our candidates didn't come to us looking for a friend, either. They looked for us to provide them with a professional service (albeit free for them), just like we did when we went to our own professionals.

ARs Going to a Base

I wanted our ARs, especially the non-military ones, to physically go on a military base. These visits enabled our people to get a visual picture and an understanding of the military that they would not have been able to acquire any other way. I also wanted them to read 100 of the military resumes we had on file, identify anything they didn't know or understand, and then ask a CR about those things, so they would learn.

New AR Advantage

When I did training with new ARs, who I knew were concerned about competing not only with our own people, but with our competition, I would tell them they had a singular advantage over people with experience. I would then ask them what they thought it was. I would typically get answers like enthusiasm, energy and hustle, which were certainly true. However, I told them their biggest advantage was they hadn't screwed up yet. Most often they didn't understand what I meant. I explained to them that every single AR who has been in this business for any length of time, has made mistakes and had candidates who did not work out.

The clients seldom blamed themselves, but instead held the recruiter responsible. That made people who had been in the business for a long time vulnerable. New people were clean, and often people think the new person may very well be better than what they have now. And, every experienced client was once a new eager person. They could identify with somebody starting out and hustling. They liked the energy and enthusiasm of somebody who wasn't taking their business for granted. My goal was to give them confidence.

CHAPTER 19

Business Things

Bringing in Minority Owners

In 2002, we brought in our four senior managers as minority owners. Despite the fact that we had a virtual talent farm at BMI, with 26 of the 100+ people at the time of my retirement being service academy graduates (which I'm pretty sure is a higher percentage than any company or even military unit, including the academies, on the planet), it was striking that of the six people who ran BMI, only two were service academy graduates (TJ Morelli and me). Each one was a superstar. All were great CRs who had formed the leadership backbone of the company. Each was well respected by our people and it made sense to bring them into the fold. Each had a rock star military record. All were athletes and all, while unique in their own ways, had superior interpersonal skills. All were already running major operations within the company.

The profiles of each:

- Wes Reel – Navy Helicopter Pilot. Admiral's Aide. Owned record for candidates attending an HC. Decorated pilot in Desert Storm. Founding Father of Enlisted recruiting at BMI.

- TJ Morelli – West Point baseball player. Academic star. Started and built Austin Office. Army Combat Engineer. Interviewed with 10 companies when he attended our HC as a candidate. All 10 badly wanted him. A rare achievement.

- Craig Griffin – Army Helicopter Pilot. Meritorious Service Medal as a young Captain. Finalist for Aide-de-camp to Commanding General of 101st Airborne Division. Owned record for most Navy Nukes at an HC. Created BMI IT/Telecom Division.
- Tim Best – Army Warrant Officer. Special Operations Helicopter Pilot. Completed college while on active duty. One of the youngest mission qualified pilot in the history of Task Force 160 (the aviation arm of Special Operations). Built the Norfolk Office.

It was obvious early in their BMI careers that each was a special talent. Consequently, as we expanded and grew, they were given the opportunity to create a separate Discipline or start and build a new office, which they did magnificently. None was more important than Wes Reel. He was the first to show it could be done and done successfully. He created our Enlisted Discipline, which grew into the largest and most successful operation, not only within BMI, but also in all of military recruiting. While none of the others reported directly to him, he served as a mentor to each, and, in no small measure, helped make their success possible. An extraordinary leader, he also was a major reason for the BMI culture to permeate throughout the company, even as we added locations and Disciplines. He also was the person I could always count on to give me tough feedback and shoot straight with me. If he thought some idea I came up with was crazy, he let me know. I valued this as much as anything he ever did. He, as much as anybody, was responsible for the success BMI enjoyed.

Bringing them in was one of the smartest things we ever did. They were now called Principals. This was our bench and gave us flexibility, as jobs and responsibilities among them changed, and were adjusted fairly often. The biggest advantage was we now had proven blue-chippers who were cooking in the same pot as Sandy and me and truly shared our perspective when decisions were made.

Scholarships and Charitable Contributions

Sandy and I created $10,000 scholarships to be awarded to students from the high schools we had attended. This was harder to do than it might seem, as our attorney had to create a trust for us to be able to select the students ourselves. We were able to go to our high schools and present the scholarships in front of an assembly on Awards Night. My dad was able to be there when I presented mine. When the recession of 2001-2004 hit, we had to discontinue them, but there was enough money put aside to cover those scholarships we had already awarded.

We also allotted each other $1,000 annually to donate as we saw fit to charities of our choice. This saved us from having to go to each other for approval, which was a hassle. While I allowed my people to bring their children's school fundraisers into work, I never brought in those of my children. I never wanted my people to feel pressure to contribute to my own.

Expansion – New Locations

Our criteria for adding an office was simple. The new office needed to be in a location that would increase the number of placements we made. Proximity to a military population, so we could more easily meet the candidates as well as get them to attend our HCs, was a major consideration. As candidates would frequently drive to our HCs, anything beyond a 300-mile distance was a deterrent for their attendance. Being located near a concentration of potential clients was important, but the size and capability of the local airport was more important. Clients would travel to attend our HCs, and an airport with direct flights from many locations made a difference.

A major consideration was our ability to attract the caliber of people we wanted at BMI. While not every location graded well in every single category, each was viewed as among the most desirable places in the U.S. to live, with the exception of Norfolk. While a nice place, it is not viewed nationally in the same way as Atlanta, San Diego, Austin and Chicago. However, the Norfolk area had unique characteristics, including a huge high-quality military population, a low cost of living and a poor nongovernment industrial base, which gave us the pick of the litter when it came to hiring our own people.

We funded our new offices with money generated from our existing operations. The most important decision we made was who we assigned to start the office. It is one thing to run an office and another to build one. While not as difficult as creating a company, it is close. You never really know how somebody will perform in that situation until they are in it. We had a 60 percent success rate which, while not ideal, was still pretty good.

Personal Umbrella Policy

I had never known something like a personal umbrella (liability) policy even existed. When I learned what it was, I made sure I took out a policy for myself. As successful as BMI was, if anything happened on my property or in my personal life, it wouldn't take long for the dots to be connected, and I would be viewed as a prime target. While nothing ever happened, it was nice to know I had this coverage if anything ever did.

Employees versus Independent Contractors

Our people were full-time employees with medical/dental, a 401k and expenses and operating costs paid to support their efforts. On occasion, we had people who wanted to be independent contractors instead of BMI employees. I suppose there would have been some benefits to them being independent contractors. (There certainly were financial benefits for us, including not having to pay for benefits and payroll taxes.) However, the team concept was too integral to our operation for us to have it any other way. We wanted our people to have an identity with the company and to need us and us them. This also meant we owned the relationships with the clients and candidates. Had our people been independent, they could have "chosen" to work with us, but not be required to do so.

Vendors

Once you determine vendors are good enough, the real question becomes how important are you to THEIR business. Are they so big that even though they do a great job, you simply aren't very important to them? You can feel this when it happens. We had to guard against that sentiment creeping in with our own clients. Although my people were so hungry, and so scarred from the startup period, they seldom took any client for granted. Too many times, they had seen the big client dry up or the small client suddenly become a big one. I remember what it felt like when I was at TLG and we held our HCs at one of the flagship Atlanta hotels. With conventions in town and staying at the same hotel, we were small-time, and we felt like it. When we needed flexibility or some accommodations, they wouldn't adjust to our needs. We were a nice piece of business for a hotel to have, but not anything that was going to be a difference maker for a hotel that size. When we started BMI and went to the Sheraton, which was smaller, the difference was obvious from the start. We also had long-term relationships with our printer, CPA, attorney and many others. However, when we felt we were being taken for granted, we made a change.

BMI's Other Businesses

As time went on, there were non-recruiting businesses we entered into, none of which I thought were very important or were difference makers. This was a source of some tension, as I finally acquiesced in approving most of them because the enthusiasm for them and the effort to not do them became a distraction itself. Not that they didn't have some benefit, but my concern was they didn't impact the mother ship (The BMI Placement Machine) that was providing the fuel and money for everything else. I was also concerned that expectations for each of these businesses were unrealistic, and even if those expectations were met, they would not come remotely close to producing what the BMI recruiting effort did.

One of these businesses was an event planning company. On paper this made sense, as we were already using another company to manage all of our HC hotel relationships. They were getting a 10 percent premium from the hotels for every dollar spent on hotel rooms under our name. The problem was, we now had to pay the person heading this new venture, and setting it up took time. It never made much money, but it did indirectly lead to our future testimony before the U.S. Senate Committee on Veterans Affairs. (More on this later.)

We also created a resume service. This was a side business I didn't think would make much money, but the product was unbelievably good. I saw the before and after with my own eyes, and was blown away with how much just one resume had been improved. The money in this world came from preparing resumes for the federal government, which on average are 10- page long documents. (I couldn't believe it either.) Our people became certified to prepare those, as well as create standard resumes. For awhile, we had this service create the resumes for Key Candidates for free, which was a nice touch. The downside was the candidates then didn't have to invest the time to prepare their own resume, but the upside was the packaging was better when we presented the candidates to our clients.

The bigger issue came when we started a job fair company along with creating a searchable database of those candidates BMI did not actively pursue. A job fair is markedly different in operation from the finely tuned and extremely detailed HC, where every single interview was scrutinized for every client and candidate. Also, as BMI worked with predominantly technical Officer and Enlisted candidates, it made sense to develop a database for candidates who needed jobs that wouldn't duplicate what BMI was already doing.

There was a business to be had in running job fairs, and with the many candidates BMI wasn't capable of helping, this was a natural way to help feed attendees to those job fairs. The problem was both of these operations were significantly different from each other, and BMI's services cost clients a lot more than attending a job fair did.

As we already had enough challenges getting East Coast ARs to sell BMI to West Coast clients, or getting them to sell a new Discipline to their current clients, there was no way they were going to sell this. Many of our ARs thought their clients might actually get some candidates from the job fairs, and then not need them as much as they had. They also worried their client relationships might be damaged by introducing "non-BMI" people to them, over whom they had little control. Now the fact that our clients could go to job fairs outside of BMI didn't get in the way of our people thinking that. They just didn't want to help it along, and hurt themselves in the process. As a result, the teamwork that had been a hallmark of BMI was never created between the two operations, even though they were physically located in the same offices.

Personal Guarantees

This is scary and something you never get used to doing. We transitioned from a small executive suite where we paid rent but, as most of the companies there were startups, a personal guarantee was not required. If you didn't pay the rent, they would just boot you out. Signing a long-term office lease is different. When we moved from our executive suite, we were able to get a really good deal to sublease office space on the first floor of the Atlanta Galleria. However, this was during the Savings and Loan fueled recession of 1991-1992, and there had been a lot of tenants who had burned commercial landlords. When we signed our new lease, we had to personally guarantee it. Not only did Sandy and I have to sign the lease, but our spouses did as well. This was sobering, and something I never forgot. This is when you truly start to understand what entrepreneurial risk is. I also learned what the term individual and collective guarantee means. While it appears on paper that if two people sign the lease each will pay 50 percent, what it really means is that if one party doesn't pay their share, the other one is still on the hook for 100 percent of it.

Employment Contracts

Our employment contracts focused on preventing people from taking our clients and candidates with them, or calling on them if they left BMI and started their own military recruiting firm. This was the standard we held ourselves to regarding TLG clients and candidates for our first year in business. We felt it was fair for us to expect the same from any of our people who left us to start their own competing firm. While we only twice had people leave us to start their own military recruiting firms, and neither company is still in business, they operated within the expected guidelines, and we had no legal issues. State laws vary, and there is debate on the enforceability of these contracts. In general, the more specific and limited they are, the more they are recognized by the courts.

The much better way was to ensure your people felt they had a good deal, were happy and wouldn't leave. The real threat for people who left and did things they shouldn't do, was we could unleash our attorney and make them run the meter on their own attorney, which would cost them money they typically didn't have. This was a threat to us in the early days, even though we didn't go after the TLG clients, and was a reason we purchased the candidate billet mailout structure from them, even though it would have been very easy for me to create it myself.

Indemnification

When I retired from BMI, one of the really important things for me was to be released and indemnified from all of my personal guarantees. I wasn't sure how this would go, but as we were in great financial shape at the time of my retirement, it wasn't a problem.

Life Insurance

We created a life insurance trust in the event Sandy, one of the principals, or I died. This would cover the amount, or much of the amount, owed by the corporation to pay for their stock in the event of death.

Standardized Fee Agreements

Our fees were either a negotiated percentage based on the first year's salary or could be a flat fee. There was also a guarantee that protected the client in the event the candidate resigned or was terminated during the guarantee period. Something many people, and certainly many military candidates, don't understand is that our fee was never subtracted from their starting salary. Companies have a pot of money that covers recruiting, and includes running ads, paying for travel, hiring in-house recruiters, or even paying recruiting firm fees. Obviously, they will save money if they don't have to pay firms like BMI, but the salary for candidates who come from recruiting firms isn't any less than for those who don't.

Negotiating fees was always a challenge, and ARs, especially new ones, had to be protected from themselves. As cold callers, they often had a beggar's mentality, and would give away the farm just to get business. We mitigated this by having some minimums based on volume of hires, exclusivity as the only military recruiting firm being used, ease of placement, brand name of the company, and how committed the company was to actually hiring military people.

We also required senior officer approval for exceptions. Holding the line on fees was a difficult thing to do, as the ever present 400-pound gorilla was ensuring we had sufficient numbers of companies to attract the candidates, and vice versa, to make the Hiring Conferences a success. This was truly a chicken-and-egg situation, which created anxiety that never really went away. Also, because we were working with so many clients, including different divisions of the same company and even different locations within the same division, we created a Master Fee Agreement Program to keep track of all of the contracts, so we knew the current fee, as well as the history.

Bank

In the late '90's, we made the decision to obtain a line of credit. We didn't really need it, as we were flush with cash, but we were in position to get one. It seemed like a good idea to gain access to money and prove our ability to repay. It was also nice to have as insurance, in case we ever needed to use it.

The bank people came out, and along with them came Hugh Long, head of Wachovia in Atlanta. He was a heavy hitter and maybe, as a Virginia Military Institute graduate and former Army Field Artillery Officer, he was intrigued by what we did. I was very impressed by him, and we hit it off. He was the first person to ever ask me, "Why do you do what you do?" Whatever answer I gave seemed to satisfy him. Then I asked him, "Why are YOU here? We are small potatoes compared to the big companies you deal with." He said they wanted to establish and develop relationships with companies that looked to have a promising future, and they felt we were one of them. This relationship would prove crucial in the years ahead.

During the recession of 2001-2004, we needed them and thank goodness we had established that relationship. In addition to the line of credit, we were able to get a bank loan to help us get through the tough times. However, this was a demand note, which meant if the bank saw we might have trouble with repayment or receivables dipped under a certain amount, they could call the note, which would have been disastrous. This note also had individual and collective personal guarantees. I had a substantial amount of money saved, and always viewed that cash as the last line of defense for the company, but this remained something I never really got used to.

Eyebrow Guy

While the bank loaned us money in 2001-2002, it was a different group that showed up in 2003-2004 to figure out how, and if, we were going to be able to pay it back. I had just finished reading a Tom Wolfe book called "A Man in Full," which is the fictional story of an Atlanta commercial real estate developer, who gets in over his head and eventually has everything come crashing down around him. What really hit me hard was the reason he was in such a dire situation was because he had personally guaranteed all of his bank loans, just like we had. Part of the book describes the workout team from the banks, which is tasked with monitoring and ensuring that companies in trouble can actually repay their loans. If they can't, this team is in position to collect the collateral from the personal guarantees. In the book, the workout people even had their collateral trophies mounted in their offices. Their trophies included Rolex watches, one of which I happened to be wearing at the time.

They came in and terrified us. The team leader guy was fairly young and had bushy eyebrows. I called him Eyebrow Guy. We (Sandy) had to submit weekly reports to him, to ensure we could pay the bank back. Now, in addition to all of the issues surrounding not having enough sales and where that was taking us, we had the additional threat of being destroyed personally because we had personally guaranteed the loans. Fun times.

One of the things I think both Sandy and I did exceptionally well during that time was to not pass on our stress and worry to our people. We never talked about our own fear or our own personal situation with any of our people. While they were well aware of our sales situation, we kept a positive attitude and moved forward with ways to improve and attack.

Layoffs

In 2003, and while we had already cut costs to the bone, we also laid off four office support people. This killed me. I felt personally responsible for them. They were innocent victims of what I felt were my bad decisions. We successfully helped three of them find follow-on positions, and while one just vanished, I felt good about at least helping three of the four land well.

U.S. Senate Testimony

The opportunity to provide U.S. Senate testimony came about as a result of Jen Hines, who ran our event planning company, having a relationship with a staffer on Capitol Hill. We were asked to provide comment on a couple of bills that would enable for profit firms like ours to have access and approval to go on military bases in the same way the nonprofit operations already had.

Our testimony was followed by questions from the Senators. We were lucky enough to follow a man whose testimony went too long, and who actually told the Senators he wasn't finished, when they more or less cut him off. It was a pretty good feeling to know we couldn't do any worse than that guy. When it was our turn, I started talking, and as my voice is already pretty loud, it was amplified by the microphones and shook the room. I got a laugh when I said I typically didn't need a microphone. Prior to going to DC, we had practiced and practiced, and tried to anticipate the questions we might get, so it went a lot easier than we thought it might.

Sandy and I rotated talking throughout our statement, and the questions were easy. Senator James Webb (D-VA) asked us if we placed Enlisted people. When I told him we placed more Enlisted than Officers, he really responded and liked that. He talked about when his brother came home from Vietnam, and used a government program to help veterans find jobs that was pretty much useless. Webb was a USNA grad, former Secretary of the Navy, one of the most highly decorated Marines of the Vietnam War, and one of my heroes. Sandy and I were able to arrange a picture with him afterwards, which was a treat. While testifying, I couldn't help but think, regardless of their politics, the Senators were among the best their states had to offer, and it was certainly an honor and a highlight to be in their presence.

While there we also met our Georgia Senator Saxby Chambliss and one of his staffers gave us a tour of the House of Representatives. We were able to walk down on the House floor, and since they were not in session, I walked up to the Speaker's podium and hit it with the gavel. Sophomoric I know, but still a pretty neat thing to do.

Acquisition of CDC

In 2007, things came full circle for us, and we acquired Career Development Corporation (CDC), which was one of the original military recruiting firms, and one that had set the bar for me on how to conduct myself in our industry. They were one of the early players in the military recruiting industry, had a great reputation, and were culturally a great fit. They were great guys and had been through it all, including the early 1980s, when that recession nearly destroyed our entire industry. We had gotten to know them really well, as a result of the GE initiative. In reality, CDC had their moment to grow like we had and chose not to. Hence, they basically created jobs for themselves (albeit well-paying jobs), but the company pretty much only consisted of the four owners, along with their great name. They were getting older, and obviously were not going to grow the business by hiring a bunch of new people. They were folded into the Norfolk Office, with a remarkably easy integration.

CHAPTER 20

Random Thoughts

My Three Biggest Mistakes

• Our first expansion location was San Diego. I really thought San Diego was the place to go first, instead of Texas, which was our other option. One of the primary reasons was that the level of competition in California was a lot less than what it was on the East Coast or in the Texas area. That, combined with the concentration of military bases in Southern California, along with the strong California economy, proved enticing. Maybe my ambition got the best of me, and it just felt good to be truly national. While we did not expect our clients to have the same people who had attended our Atlanta HCs attend those in San Diego, we did assume our track record of success with those clients would pave the way for us to establish relationships with their counterparts located in or near California. However, the time zone differential, with having our HQ and already established ARs physically located on the East Coast, proved problematic. The window for having actual phone conversations, with lunch factored in on both ends, was half what it was for those in the same time zone.

As a result, our East Coast operation wasn't much help in getting San Diego off of the ground, and the client relationships had to be developed from scratch, which slowed down everything. It also would have been better, as it was our first true expansion, to not have it located 3,000 miles away. Eventually, this office became successful, but not going to Texas first, made it harder than it needed to be.

With our Enlisted Discipline so successful, we looked to add other areas to recruit. We created an IT/Telecom operation that was very successful. The military does everything with computers except create the software, and had high-tech communications well before the civilian world. The expertise was there in both areas. This Discipline had a great multi-year run that ended with the dotcom implosion of 2001.

> After having three Disciplines that worked, we added our fourth, which was Medical. We targeted the technicians and nurses. As the candidate and client numbers would never be enough to provide enough interviews and make attending an HC worthwhile, we created a virtual HC format where the interviews took place en masse over the telephone on pre-scheduled days. We made placements and things looked like they were going in the right direction. However, the falloff rate (candidates changing their mind about taking the offer after having accepted the position, not showing up on the first day of work, or not lasting the guaranteed period) was almost 50 percent. We couldn't believe it. The candidates were accepting positions and then knowing where they were going to live, would contact the other hospitals in that area to see if they could make more money. As hospitals in major cities are easy to find, this wasn't hard to do.

The essence of the problem was that hospitals are almost uniform in their organizational structure and mission. Even the lingo and terminology are the same. This was different from every other client that used us, and made it easy for the candidates to do what they did. Two companies in the same city, which provide the same product or service, are often very different – if they could even be located. Hospitals were virtually identical. I failed to recognize that.

• When I was at TLG, I hired somebody for a key area, even though my instincts were screaming at me not to hire him. I really needed to fill the position, and other people were telling me he was a fit. But something inside me was telling me not to do it. I vividly remember before he was hired, being at a party with him and he couldn't, or wouldn't, participate in charades. I thought how odd that was; what kind of sales guy won't play charades? Anyway, the need to get somebody onboard caused me to go against my instincts, and I hired him. It turned out to be a big mistake, which happened because I didn't listen to myself. I learned a valuable lesson, and for the rest of my career, I always trusted my instincts, and they rarely let me down.

USNA Panel on Women

Sometimes you get to do neat things. I was invited to be on the panel to celebrate and discuss 30 years of women at the Naval Academy. I was a junior at the Naval Academy when the first class of women was admitted. I remember thinking how off base it was that so many of my fellow midshipmen had such an issue with women being there. I thought it was a bit much for people who hadn't graduated yet, to even have a say in who the academy admitted, as if they were somehow in charge or had enough wisdom to make that call. Besides, I felt lucky to be there in the first place. Who was I to say somebody else shouldn't be there, male or female? The women in the first class were really outstanding. However, they had it rough. All of their male classmates could blend in with the other male members of the class, whereas anything the women did wrong, real or imagined, was easily noticed. I had a great deal of respect for them and still do.

When the time came for me to speak, I said, "I was a member of the Class of '78 that gave all of you such a warm welcome when you arrived 30 years ago." This broke the ice and got a good laugh. Janie Mines, USNA '80, was running the program. She was very impressive. God knows why I was there, but they wanted me to talk about issues facing female academy graduates who were transitioning out of the military. It went well. The next day, Captain Wendy Lawrence, USNA '81, and a then current astronaut, gave a Forrestal Lecture to the entire brigade, which was great. She was the daughter of Vice Admiral William Lawrence, who was a long-serving POW, test pilot, and former Academy Superintendent.

Entrepreneur's Mindset

It dumbfounds me when people who are not entrepreneurs talk about the entrepreneurial spirit, and how they think the tax code is driving entrepreneurship. When we started, the tax code wasn't even on our radar. Worrying about the tax code was way down the line. I know my thought was if I have to pay a lot of taxes, then I'm probably making a lot of money. I doubt most founders of companies are too worried about tax rates when they start or even know that much about them. They have a dream to start a company and make it successful. Maybe we were atypical because we had saved our money, funded the company out of our own savings and never took on investors. While we grew past what would be considered a small business, when you start out in a 250-square-foot executive suite, you never really forget it. I suppose like Depression-era children who never forget, neither did I. My thought process and mindset were always that of the small businessman.

Obviously, an awareness of tax rates became a factor as we expanded and grew. And undoubtedly, investors factor anticipated capital gains tax rates into their decision to invest. But when BMI opened in 1991, it wasn't much of a consideration for me.

Somebody Else's Dime

Starting a company is hard, and you better know what you're doing before you launch. As there is really no way to know how to run a company until you are in the saddle, you better know how to make money. You also must be sure you are really passionate about the business itself. I was fortunate in that I knew from my time at TLG, how to generate placements and that I loved the business. I also made mistakes while there, and learned from them. Despite the fact I had experience in running a national military recruiting operation while at TLG, there was a litany of things I learned only after we launched BMI.

There are no shortcuts in running a business. I would advise anyone who is thinking of starting a company to first work for a company in that industry. Learn and make mistakes on somebody else's dime, like I did. Veterans are prime targets to start franchises in just about every industry, for the same reasons they are sought by Corporate America. However, I sometimes wonder if the veterans themselves have spent enough (or any) time learning the business, or if they even like the industry, before they make that kind of commitment.

Time to Think

I spent virtually all day, every day, speaking with people, whether it was with my own employees, candidates or clients. In a people-intensive business, that was standard fare and expected. Coming home at night to five children provided little respite. However, I needed time to simply think. A couple of things I did helped. Swimming was one. As a regular, albeit slow swimmer (one mile per hour), that time enabled me to let my mind wander, think about the problems and issues of the day, and ponder the future. I also used the Christmas break, which was a slow time for us and when my people typically took vacations. With few people around, I was able to tackle projects that required my focus and undivided attention.

Second Most Important Decision

The most important decision you will make is whether to even start your company. A lot of people talk about doing it, but few do. Of those who do, most don't succeed. However, next on the list is to decide specifically what product the company will make or what service it will provide. There can be a tendency to minimize that risk by increasing the number of products, which inevitably leads to not doing anything well, or squandering your limited resources and then not having the capability to respond when a real opportunity presents itself. For us, that decision was being ultra-focused and totally committed to placing Officers in locations East of the Mississippi River into technical leadership positions. However, when you committed to a particular product or service, you better be right. What every entrepreneur knows, and makes this decision scary, is if you were wrong, you wouldn't get a second chance.

Saving Money

I learned to save money early on from my dad. He made me put half of any money I earned into the bank. You can also save a lot of money while at sea making Western Pacific deployments. When I left the Navy, I had saved $15,000, which enabled me to not have to jump into a job I didn't want to do just to have some income. While I made a lot of money when I was at TLG, it was the saving of that money that gave me the ability and freedom to help start BMI.

Mixing Personal and Business Relationships

I never felt comfortable mingling my personal and business relationships, as it tended to not work out very well. I think I felt that way because I was in the recruiting business, and there are a lot of things that can go wrong when it comes to getting people jobs. Seldom does the person looking for employment think it was their fault if it didn't work out. I had to learn this the hard way as there were people I served with who I tried to help. When things didn't work out for them, I typically didn't get a thank you for my efforts, but a feeling that somehow I was involved and should have helped them more. This was less of an issue on the client side, but I did have my people shy away from attempting to get business from a major company where my sister worked in human resources. While I never came out and said to not pursue this company, I never encouraged us to after it, so the effect was the same. I felt like a lot of things could go wrong, and didn't want to complicate my sister's life.

People Who Had to be Better

I noticed how successful some of my people were, despite not completing college. I think my people who had not finished college had an edge to prove they were just as good as those who had. I also looked for people with that mindset to perform my personal business. I had a home designer, who was not an architect, do my garage-to-office conversion, and a female construction manager build that along with finishing my basement and attic. I never forgot, and couldn't help but have been impressed by Honest John from the SBA Awards. I always took note of people who had to be better because they had something stacked against them, and tried to utilize them whenever I had the chance. This wasn't due to any charity on my part; I knew they probably were more capable just by surviving in their business.

Quality Time

I think quality time is a myth. People use that phrase as an excuse to justify not spending enough time. There is just logging time, and some of it's quality and a lot of it isn't. It is impossible to really lead people unless they know you view them as important enough to spend time with. No matter who you are, or what you do, the ultimate statement on what is truly important to you is where you spend your time.

Age 27

Women mature faster than men. How many times have we seen men, who were average students or were stars in school sports, paying little attention to something that has very little to do with a successful future, end up being rock stars in their professional lives? It's almost like the ability was there all along, but it was misdirected. Then in their mid-20s, they realize that whatever they are (or are not) doing matters, and they focus, mature and become not just good, but great. However, my experience is, if they don't get it together by age 27, they don't ever get it together. What they are by that age is pretty much what they are.

Opportunity Lost by the Military

There was an opportunity lost by the military recruiting services in not taking advantage of the fact that firms like ours existed. The services were well aware of our presence, but to acknowledge us almost seemed like an encouragement by them for people to leave the service. One of the biggest concerns parents have with their children joining the military (other than being injured or killed) is they will fall behind their peers. The reality is their military service leapfrogs them ahead. Failure to arm their recruiters with the information on what our industry could do for people when they left the service was a chance left on the table.

Enjoyed Practice More Than the Game

When I coached football, I always enjoyed the practices more than the games. I coached the offensive line, and had to teach my players what to do prior to the game. Once the game started, I wasn't going to be able to do much more than tweak things, or remind them of what I had already taught them. It was the same with the HC. At the HC, all of the prep work had been done. It was either on track to be successful or it wasn't. Coaching was very similar to running the company. It was process and teamwork, getting the right people into the right positions, and having them play with confidence. A different age group to be sure, but the fundamentals were very similar.

Assessment Tools

I have a fairly healthy skepticism for assessment tests. Part of this comes from my own experiences with candidates who I knew were great fits for the clients, but for whatever reason, did not provide the right answers on the mandatory tests. When I was at TLG, there was a test given over the phone by a company, which assessed a potential hire's communication ability. One particular person taking the test had a somewhat herky-jerky communication style, and ended up with the lowest possible passing score. In fact, it was so low that my boss had to fight to hire him. This was no average person. He was a West Pointer, Honor Graduate of Ranger School and, while stationed in Germany, not only had the top-scoring tank platoon in all of Germany, but his own tank had the highest firing scores. Think about that. Of all of the tanks in Germany at that time, his was the best. He went on to be, in my opinion, the greatest CR our industry has ever seen. So much for barely passing. The tools are just a tool.

Pedigree

Within our company, pedigree might help you get an interview, but that was about all. I was a lot more interested in what people had done outside of school than what they had done in it. Once a person started with us, their previous rank or where they went to college might make interesting conversation, but not much more. At BMI, former Commissioned Officers were working for prior Enlisted people, and a former Army Warrant Officer was leading a lot of academy graduates.

Humor in Stupid Stuff

I always saw the humor in the stupid and ridiculous stuff my people did in the Navy. I felt the same with my people at BMI. I used to tell my people that if they did something stupid, to make sure it was stupid and funny, so at least we would then have a story to tell. We had a candidate who gave us some referrals, so one of my people told him to treat himself to a dinner, and we would pay for it. He neglected to get approval from Sandy and, worse, didn't give him a dollar limit on what we would pay. This guy decided to take his wife out to the finest restaurant in Chicago (Mickey Trotter's) for their anniversary dinner. When we got the reimbursement request for more than $300, it didn't go down very well, but at least we had a story.

We also had a client who gave the Wunderlic Test to the candidates they were interviewing. This was a version of the famous test given to prospective college football players in advance of the NFL draft, which supposedly tests their basic intelligence. Our AR decided to take the test to see how he would do. Soon enough, word spread around the company and others were taking it as well. (I took the test, too.) It seemed like a cool thing to see how we compared to NFL prospects. Nobody realized there was a charge for every test taken. When we got a bill for $4,000, it didn't seem quite as cool.

Recessions

While it might seem counterintuitive, I think the best time to start a business is during a recession. (I have been through three of them, having started with TLG in 1987, launching BMI in 1991, in addition to enduring 2001-2004.) During that time, you are making your way, figuring out what to do and how to do it, and aren't really in a position to take advantage of a good market. Besides, you're not getting much business anyhow, because you're so new. When the economy turns, you are then in position to take advantage of it. A lot of startup companies try to catch the wave, and start their business when things are going great. The problem is they still suffer from being new, and probably aren't getting much business because of that. When things turn south, they are in position to get the business but, unfortunately, there is now a lot less business to be had.

Economists will debate all of the reasons, but I think recessions are the inevitable price paid for natural human optimism and judgment failures. You had better have things in place to make it through one. Money is one of them, but so is having goodwill on deposit with your people and your clients, as well as having the ability to be flexible and make good decisions.

Nobody in their right mind would ever recommend going through a recession, but there are positives if you survive and come out the other end relatively intact. The competitive landscape tends to be a lot cleaner. Weaker competitors have likely vanished, and there is more business for those companies that remain in existence. Your company and your people will be better, more committed and have shown they will stick through the tough times.

At USNA

In 1974, my Class ('78), which numbered 1,515, was the largest class to ever enter the Naval Academy before or since. We ended up graduating 943 – an attrition rate of almost 40 percent. The Academy was hard and demanding. There were many times I wanted to quit. However, as I had never quit anything before, I really didn't know how. I also knew staying the course would be worth it. You learn many things by going through an intense experience like this. One of the most important is learning how to endure, tough it out and make the best of whatever situation you are facing.

I vividly remember days where you were nailed at morning inspection for your uniform not being squared away, then going to class and having a pop quiz you weren't ready for, and then blowing a major test for which you had really studied hard. While you were at class your room was inspected and found wanting. It wasn't even lunchtime yet, and the day had already been a disaster. At that point, you really had a choice. You could allow the rest of the day to continue on its downward trajectory and bury you, or you could dig in and make the rest of the day a good one. I learned to compartmentalize and focus on the next task and do my best to not have what had previously happened occur again.

I never much got into the inspections, rules and hazing of the academy. I did what I had to do, but knew that if I didn't make it to graduation, it would be because of grades. I surprised myself with my grades, and soon enough realized I was just as smart or smarter than a lot of my classmates, who had graduated from elite prep schools or were at the top of their high school classes.

Prior to going, I was scared to death about flunking plebe chemistry. While I had good College Board scores, I had received a C in high school chemistry, and knew I didn't know or understand it. So, I arranged to get some tutoring before I went. When the academy placement exams were administered a couple of weeks into Plebe Summer, having just been exposed to chemistry, I scored higher than people who had taken it as sophomores in high school, but had forgotten more than I knew. The first day of chemistry class, I walked into class only to learn I was in higher-level chemistry with people who were talking about majoring in chemistry. It was like an episode out of the Twilight Zone - my worst nightmare.

Struggling through the semester, I got a lifeline for the midterm exam. The professor said he was going to take 50 questions out of a book of 500 multiple-choice questions. I knew this was my chance to stay afloat, so I memorized 500 answer groups. I didn't even look at the questions. When the test came, he was good for his word, and there in front of me were 50 questions from that book. I knew the answer to every one. Then I realized I could give myself a grade of 100, but if I did, he might think I cheated or had somehow stolen the exam, so I gave myself a 92. Sometimes I have wondered what grade I could have earned, if I had actually studied the course material that hard. However, having a different way to solve a problem was to my advantage. Just like going into the stands to sell peanuts instead of trying to sell where the large groups were, I looked at things differently. I think this different way of viewing things, led in some way, to becoming an entrepreneur.

USNA Heartbreak

Prior to our 20 year class reunion, our class president wanted to locate all of the members of our USNA class, whether they had graduated or not. In particular, he wanted to bring the non-graduates back into the fold. I was asked to do it for my company (there are 36 companies at the Naval Academy). In my company, we had graduated 27 of the 43 we started with and were able to locate 39 of the 43. Some of the conversations I had with the guys who hadn't graduated were heartbreaking. Many of them had gone on to have very successful lives, but were in purgatory about their Naval Academy experience. Some didn't feel they had even earned the right to be a part of the class because they hadn't graduated. Yet, they had made close friends there, having gone through such an intense experience together. Some had never even talked about their experience with anybody. Some felt ashamed because they had not finished. It was tough to hear their stories.

I was a four-year member of the Brigade Honor Committee. Among our duties was to serve as jury members, if somebody was accused of violating the Honor Code. This duty was assigned, so you normally didn't know the accused or know them very well. I remember the cases as typically involving somebody young doing something stupid. Hearing the angst of my company-mates who hadn't graduated reminded me of the Honor cases as well. Where do you put not only getting tossed out of a service academy, but having the reason be for committing an Honor Violation?

Veteran Unemployment

I read the statistics like everybody else, and they mystify me. We built a company placing veterans into industry and, while we focused our efforts on people with a technical background, I know other veterans were much sought after as well. So how can their unemployment rate be so high or be perceived to be so high? I know there are veterans who have severe issues, both physical and psychological, and require special help. However, I would bet the unemployment rate for a departing service member with leadership experience, or who has been in the military for any length of time, is significantly lower than that of a 22 year old after their first enlistment. Are these two distinct groups of veterans lumped together in the unemployment stats? Probably.Those young service members are no doubt a lot better than their civilian counterparts without their experience. Yet in many cases, they are still a 22 year old without any directly transferrable skills. The best thing they can do for themselves is to get some education or credentials.

I take issue with the tone of many of the veteran hiring initiatives of some of our major companies. While I think what they are doing is positive, and I suppose any large company is going to seek positive press from anywhere they can, there seems to be an element of charity in the messaging. If this is what it takes to introduce the concept of hiring veterans to Corporate America, so be it.

However, the reality is most veterans make great employees. I bristle at the suggestion they might only be hired as part of a charitable outreach program, instead of because they are simply that good. What is really stunning is of today's 18-24 age cohort, only 29 percent of them would even be eligible to join the military due to a failure to graduate from high school, having a criminal record, prior drug use, or medical or physical limitations.[4] How then, can those who are able to make the military's cut, combined with the extensive training and experience they received while in the military, not be viewed as the very job candidates to be recruited and hired by every company in the country?

The other thing I wonder about is the entire infrastructure the state and federal government, as well as the nonprofits, have set up to help veterans find employment. Every single one of these programs is designed to help the transitioning veteran find a job, but at the end of the day, the only one who is really accountable for making it happen is the veteran. Wes Reel, he of the Enlisted Recruiting Program at BMI, had the idea long ago for

---

[4] Department of Defense, QMA Study 2013

the government to just allot money to us, and only pay us when we found the veteran a job. Pay for performance. Human nature is such that there is a difference between wanting to make something happen and being paid only when it happens.

The Bear

Two men are in a campsite. A bear appears and looks like it might attack. One man starts to run away. The other one goes into the tent to put on his running shoes. The first one yells to the other, "What are you doing, putting on your shoes? You can't outrun that bear!" The one in the tent yells back, "I don't have to outrun the bear. I just have to outrun you."

Notwithstanding the lack of heroism in helping his mate, the moral of the story is the winner is often the person who simply does one more thing. I constantly thought I had to do one more thing. Whether it was making one more call to a candidate, sending one more handwritten note to a client, doing one more extra thing to help one of my people, or following through on a host of other things, I never lost that feeling. I'm sure some of that stems from not being a "golden boy" myself. I felt I had to do extra. I know doing "one more thing" made a difference to the success I had personally, and that BMI had as a company.

Prior History with People

I think it is very hard to start a company with people you have worked with previously. Your roles may now be different, which can upset whatever chemistry you had before. This is one of the reasons why I didn't want TLG people along with me when we started BMI. Although Sandy and I had worked in the same building, we had actually never worked together. This was a negative in some respects, as we had to get used to working together, and it took time to sort out our different responsibilities. However, we also started fresh.

Control of Operations

One of the reasons we were successful was because we controlled all of the important things. Our people were employees, and we made our own product. We had our own sales force. We physically worked together in offices, and we had our own money (until much later). We also built our own software. I had a friend who owned a technology company that failed. While he owned the patents and the manufacturing process on how his equipment was made, he also had some stumbling blocks. He had investors, the actual manufacturing was done at a place he didn't control, and he used manufacturing reps to sell for him. He had a pretty good product, but just didn't control enough things himself. He was too dependent on others.

How to Leave a Company

I have seen too many people leave companies, and then talk poorly about the company with the people who were still there. Oftentimes it felt like a divorce, where they wanted somebody to agree with them about how bad their spouse was. The people still on the team don't want to hear it. While they may agree with the opinion, it's never OK for somebody who is no longer on the team to bash it. Eventually, those friendships go by the wayside. It's the responsibility of the person who leaves to never talk poorly about what they left behind. I always took great pride in how I left TLG. Those relationships were, and remain, important to me to this day.

Cutting Words

On our ship, my group did the Vertreps[5] and prior to their operation, we always did a prebrief to review what would happen and when. One time we were late to the prebrief and it was my fault, and the prebrief was not as good as it normally was. The Air Boss, a Navy Captain and former

---

[5] Vertical Replenishment. Helicopters transport pallets of supplies and deliver them onto the flight deck. Can be done at sea or inport.

fighter squadron commanding officer, controlled all flight operations on our aircraft carrier and was a great man. He pulled me aside after the Vertrep and told me, "I thought you were better than that." Cutting words that were a lot worse than any chewing out he might have given me. Another time, we had a visiting Admiral go through our berthing spaces, and they weren't up to snuff. Our Ship's Executive Officer (second in command of a nuclear aircraft carrier who would go on to make Admiral) called my Master Chief and me into his office. He said, "I thought you were guys I could count on." When I left the Navy, he actually held up my resignation paperwork, hoping I would change my mind. When I told him teaching was in my plans, he said, "No way. You'll be an entrepreneur." Prescient.

I never forgot how horrible I felt after failing two people, whose approval I wanted. If they had yelled at me, it would have been a lot easier. I never forgot the feeling of letting them down. When I needed to make an impression on someone about something they should have done better, I always tried to communicate that they had disappointed me. I never raised my voice. Never.

Social Media

Clearly, the advent of social media has changed the recruiting game. Anything that increases the ability of a recruiter to find, qualify, and contact potential clients or candidates is a good thing. Also, the ease of communication simply makes coordinating interviews and providing information easier. These are obvious. The real danger is to think technology can equate or replace the need for a personal relationship between the client, recruiter and candidate.

More efficient doesn't always mean better. Recruiting by email is not much different than leading by email. It doesn't work. Time has to be spent in person and on the telephone developing the relationship. Electronic communication, in all of its forms, can help facilitate things, but it will never build the relationship. I don't believe recruiting is a transactional business. Life's major decisions, such as buying a house, where to go to college, and signing up for the military, are not made without a baseline of trust having been developed with someone in a position to provide guidance and information. Making the decision on where to go to work is no different.

Of all of the various social media platforms that currently exist, I think LinkedIn is unique. I gave a talk recently to the Atlanta Chapter of the Naval Academy Alumni Association, and described a LinkedIn profile as being akin to the uniform we all wore while in the military. A LinkedIn profile provides a quick overview of who you are, where you've been, and what you've done. A military uniform with its rank insignia, medals and badges does the same. Now achievers and successful people can have their background and accomplishments "checked out," without having to do the self-promotion.

Shaun G. Bradley

CHAPTER 21

Other Anecdotes

CIA

One of the strangest things that happened to us at BMI was just after we had moved into our new offices. We were approached by a middle-aged lady who was with the CIA (she showed us her identification). They wanted to be able to use our company by having people work for us, while they were transitioning from wherever they were coming from to wherever they were going. This apparently is not that uncommon, but it was new for us. The whole thing seemed pretty crazy. We weren't given much information on who the people would be, or anything else for that matter.

While we would never be forced to do anything we didn't agree with, the entire thing was vague, and we didn't sense the CIA really understood what we did. Hence, we decided to not do it. While we were certainly patriotic and listened, this just seemed too far out there for us to monkey with. I could only imagine what it would have been like in our small company of, back then fewer than 10 people, having some person, who was from another country and might barely speak English, suddenly "working" for us.

Our Initial Furniture

In the beginning to save money, we bought a mixed collection of furniture and desks from a major commercial office developer, who was getting rid of it. I think it was cheaper for him to sell it to us than to move it. The joke in the office was that our furniture all matched – just not each other.

Disney Cruise in 2003

I had a singular experience in 2003, while on a Disney cruise. We had purchased this vacation years earlier when the business was going great, so the cruise was already paid for, but times were brutal. I remember seeing my family seated for dinner and, as I was walking towards the table, thought, "I hope to God you all are enjoying it, because it may never happen again." During this period, I also remember looking at my house from the yard and, as everything had been personally guaranteed, wondering whether we would still be living in this house the next year.

Merlin Olsen

I learned many things from Rear Admiral Mitchell, but one I never forgot was his story about Merlin Olsen, the Hall of Fame Los Angeles Rams defensive tackle. He was at a function and Olsen was there, standing by himself. People knew who he was, because by this time he was also a famous star on television. However, the people there were too intimidated to come up and talk to him. Rear Admiral Mitchell introduced himself, and Olsen was appreciative. Olsen said, "Thank you for coming over to say hello. I don't know anybody here, and it's nice to have somebody to talk to." So here is this famous football player and actor, and people just assumed things that weren't there. It takes nothing to say hello to somebody. I never forgot this.

Balance

I can be pretty intense. I remember one of my people telling me in the early days, "Shaun, you need more balance in your life." I told him, "Let me tell you what balance means to me. Balance means being the best in business AND being the best husband AND the best father." Whenever I hear the word balance, I hear an excuse for mediocrity. The key is to identify the important things, and then shed those things that aren't.

CHAPTER 22

My Personal Life

My wife, Libby, was a VP in another area of TLG when we dated. Our relationship was a "known secret" for a long time. (My boss knew.) Even though there was no official policy regarding fraternization, and she was a VP in a different department while I was still a frontline recruiter, we didn't want to take any chances and rock the boat. This all came to a head when Art wanted to promote me and move me to the Dallas office. A promotion I obviously turned down.

To say she had blind confidence we would be successful when we started BMI is an understatement, and contributed greatly to the success we had. Maybe because she was at TLG and saw the military group grow from nothing to what it became, I never had to deal with a spouse who wondered if I was crazy to leave TLG and start a company. Libby always believed, and her confidence in me helped give me confidence in myself. She also went back to work as a nurse to help us through the tough times in the early days.

Besides the blind confidence she had in me that we would be successful, she was a crucial factor in the success of BMI. While never involved in any of the operations of the company, she played a very, very important role. She was a very visible person, going into the office every so often, and certainly attended every company function or get-together. Libby made sure she knew the wives and husbands and knew their story. When anybody had a baby, she made sure "we" sent them a gift. When she saw the recruiters, she always made a point to tell them she knew how well they were doing, and did the same with the spouses. She knew their children. Everybody loved her and I have no doubt there were times when people gave me the benefit of the doubt, thinking I must be OK, if she married me.

Some people compartmentalize their lives. I lived the total opposite – an integrated life. I would take calls from my wife and kids at the office and dealt with BMI things at home. My people saw me do this. My children, as well as their children, were frequently in the office. Getting the job done was what was important, and the flexibility to handle personal things was never a problem for me or for them.

I never took what would be considered a true vacation from work. I made phone calls, or had conversations every day. I typically did these in the morning, and it never got in the way of our vacation. I wanted to know what was going on. More accurately, I needed to know what was going on. My wife had a background in the business, so she understood and never gave me a hard time.

We started BMI when our oldest child was seven months old. (We eventually would have five kids in six years, with at least one of them in diapers for eight years. Some were in diapers longer than others – sorry kids, you deserved that.) For the first five years of BMI's existence, I worked every day of the week, but my routine was a bit unusual, I suppose. My routine was to arrive at work around 7:30 a.m. - 8 a.m. depending on whether I was dropping my kids off at preschool. I would typically get home around 6 p.m - 6:30 p.m., eat dinner, and then give the kids their bath and put them to bed. Then I would work from 8 p.m – 10 p.m. from my house.

On Saturday mornings, I would bring my kids with me into the office, and I also worked from home on Sunday night from about 6 p.m. - 9 p.m. I found the best time to talk to candidates was during the workweek evenings, Saturday mornings or Sunday nights anyway, so this schedule worked out well for me. They were typically around and available. I realize that with today's communication technology, anybody can be contacted at any time, but that was not the case back then.

If there is anything I did that was smart, it is what I did with my children. I was the primary one to put them to bed and give them their baths. I was not raised around a bunch of children and had never babysat.

Frankly, I didn't have much confidence in what to do with children or how to do it. I also knew I needed to develop some confidence in this area. I didn't want to be the substitute, who did things only when my wife couldn't, so I carved out my own area. I wanted her to be the substitute for me. Giving baths and putting the kids to bed provided that for me. It helped give me confidence as a father that I could do it. It also had the benefit of sharing the load, but that was a by-product, not the goal, of why I did it this way.

I had pretty much stripped my life down to my family and BMI, but when my daughter turned five, it led me back to sports and coaching. I began a life outside of BMI that ultimately involved coaching every one of my children as they progressed through the various age groups in baseball, softball, basketball and football. Eventually, I coached those same sports well past when my children had either moved on from the sport or were playing in high school or college. To date, I have coached over 60 teams, from six year olds through high school. I shudder to think what my life would have missed, had I not travelled that road. Leadership is leadership, and it doesn't much change from coaching kids to being an officer in the military to running a company or being a father. However, there is certainly something special about impacting a young person's life, and sharing the same goals to help them improve and be part of a team.

One of the best parts of my coaching life has been the relationships and camaraderie with my fellow coaches. After retiring from BMI, I still had that well-developed world to be part of, which made a huge difference for me. I have read about people who suffer when they leave their team. NFL players are often profiled, but I don't believe this is unique to them. The camaraderie among the coaches, the sense of mission, along with the corresponding teamwork and leadership were really important to me. Had I not had that world in place when I retired from BMI, I might have been very lost.

CHAPTER 23

The Most Important
Things I Learned

- Will somebody pay money for your product or service? If they will, why will they buy it from you? You had better know the answer to both questions.

- Know why you're making the decisions you make. What are the underlying principles?

- The connection is everything.

- You have to be ethically clean in everything you do, all of the time.

- You have to be a subject matter expert, and be viewed that way.

- You have to love the business.

- Pay people for what they've done, not for what they're going to do.

- There is no substitute for being visible and logging the time.

- You can smile and laugh and have fun and still be successful.

- Develop a life outside of work.

- Relationships are built before you need them, not when you need them.

- Commit to a specific business niche. Focus matters, especially in the beginning.

• Starting a company will be twice as hard, cost twice as much, and take twice as long as you think it will. No matter how much or how well you plan, you had better build in a cushion for the unplanned and unexpected.

CHAPTER 24

Last Thoughts

As I re-read what I've written, it occurred to me that I might have somehow portrayed BMI as the Wild West, with inmates running the asylum. Nothing could be further from the truth. Merit mattered. Not letting your mate down mattered. Integrity mattered. We were irreverent, and anything overly formal was viewed as pretentious. It had the best elements of a locker room. I never viewed loose and laughter as being in conflict with professional and productive. In fact, I viewed them as essential ingredients. Tight and controlling can yield short-term results, but I don't think it works over the long haul. It certainly doesn't work with high-quality people. I also know that for better or worse, the BMI culture was reflected in my personality and view of the world, and we hired and attracted people who were similar.

I suppose the final judgment on any leader or owner is what was left behind when you moved on, and how the organization then performed. When I retired, I knew the talent was there and the systems, processes and culture were in place. However, you never really know what will happen. I remain proud that BMI was able to absorb the brutal hits from the financial crisis, and emerge doing things even beyond what was achieved, while I was at the helm.

Shaun G. Bradley

CHAPTER 25

Conclusion

So that is the story. I have said many times that America rewards risk more than talent, and I know that was true in my case. My timing was pretty incredible. While I was not present at the beginning of our industry, I was there when it took off, and has now in its various forms, helped tens of thousands of veterans gain positions in countless companies and organizations, where they have made a difference. In writing this book, I am reminded of how fortunate I was to have had so many positive influences in my life. From my dad making me save money, to my mom "educating" me on the difference between right and wrong, to my grandfather teaching me about loyalty, they and many others helped form me.

Being around Rear Admiral Mitchell, Coach Wall, and Master Chief Griffith was like being given the keys to the world's best leadership school. All I had to do was take it in. Art Lucas taught me how to run a business and my first boss, Carol Rifkin, showed me you could have fun in Corporate America. BMI couldn't have happened without Sandy Morris. She was the perfect complement to me in having the skills and temperament I did not. Wes Reel was the best wingman anybody has ever had. None of this comes to pass without my wife, Libby. Blind confidence does not come close to describe how much trust she had in me. I fell into a career I loved and happened to be good at. I was lucky.

Shaun G. Bradley

Glossary of Terms

- Air Wing - Operational unit assigned to an aircraft carrier composed of fixed wing aircraft and helicopter squadrons.

- AR - Account Representative. Individual responsible for establishing relationships with and managing BMI client companies.

- Billings - Each recruiter's credit for their portion of the placement fee. Commissions were then paid based on their commission rate.

- CR - Candidate Recruiter. Individual responsible for recruiting military candidates for the job openings of BMI client companies.

- CC - Conference Coordinator. Individual responsible for scheduling and managing all facets of a BMI Hiring Conference.

- CDC - Career Development Corporation. Military recruiting firm located in Alexandria, Virginia. Eventually acquired by BMI.

- Discipline - Different product lines within BMI. Over time, BMI had Disciplines in Commissioned Officers, Enlisted technicians, Medical, and IT/Telecom.

- Executive Suite - Small office space. Leases are typically for a year or less. Used by startups or companies that need occasional access to an office in a major city.

- Falloff - Unsuccessful placement. Candidate changes mind after accepting an offer, does not show up for work on the first day, or does not last through the guaranteed period.

- HC - Hiring Conference. Two-day event held at a business hotel where pre-scheduled individual interviews occurred between BMI client companies and military candidates. 600+ interviews could take place between 130+ candidates and 70+ companies.

• OC - Off-Conference. Initial interviews that occurred independent of an HC. Could occur in person or via telephone.

• Master Chief - Master Chief Petty Officer. E-9. Highest Navy enlisted rank. Enlisted ranks range from E-1 to E-9. The other military services have equivalents with different names.

• Nuke - Navy Nuclear Trained Officer. Hard science or degreed engineer from only the top colleges and universities. Receive 18 months of extensive training prior to reporting to their submarine or ship. Among the most sought after candidates.

• RADM - Rear Admiral. Navy Flag Rank. O-8. Military Commissioned Officer ranks range from O-1 to O-10, with a 4-star admiral or general the highest.

• RW - Recruiterware. Proprietary HC scheduling software that evolved into supporting candidate and client management and matching, as well as aiding with internal communications.

• TLG - The Lucas Group. National multi-discipline recruiting firm headquartered in Atlanta.

• USAFA – United States Air Force Academy. Located in Colorado Spring, Colorado. Approximately 4,000 cadets attend. Produces commissioned officers for the U.S. Air Force.

• USMA - United States Military Academy. Located in West Point, New York. Approximately 4,000 cadets attend. Produces commissioned officers for the U.S. Army.

• USNA - United States Naval Academy. Located in Annapolis, Maryland. Approximately 4,000 midshipmen attend. Produces commissioned officers for the U.S. Navy and Marine Corps.

Acknowledgements

I have newfound respect for those who write for a living. As a novice author, and somebody who has craved being part of a team or being around people my entire life, I never adjusted to the solitary aspects of writing. I was fortunate in having family and friends who encouraged me and believed in this effort. The time they took to listen to me and edit and improve my drafts was incredible. Family included my wife, Libby, niece, Jill Yeomans (my ace in the hole as a professional author), and brother-in-law, Jeff Rogers. My sister, Marla, inherited my mother's English and grammar skills, and made countless improvements. BMI alums Pam Andersen and Beth Jarvis were crucial. An army of friends provided great insight and included Frank Behm, Joe Massaro, Nancy Prochaska, Mike Rosenberg, Chuck Seigrist, Eric Stagliano and Martha Whittaker. Rachel Gray made a final, invaluable review. This book is never written without your help. Thank you.

For more information contact:

Shaun G. Bradley
C/O Advantage Books
P.O. Box 160847
Altamonte Springs, FL 32716

info@ advbooks.com

To purchase additional copies of this book or other books published by
Advantage Books call our order number at:

407-788-3110 (Book Orders Only)

or visit our bookstore website at:
www.advbookstore.com

Longwood, Florida, USA
"we bring dreams to life"™
www.advbookstore.com